CONGRESSIONAL QUARTERLY'S

CANDIDATES
'96

★ ★ ★

CONGRESSIONAL QUARTERLY'S

CANDIDATES '96

Profiles of Presidential Contenders

Ronald D. Elving,
editor

Congressional Quarterly Inc.
Washington, D.C.

Editor: Ronald D. Elving
Production Editor: Kerry Kern
Contributors: Jennifer Babson, Julie Blair, Emily Church, Rhodes Cook, Alexis DeVane, Phil Duncan, Allan Freedman, Alan Greenblatt, Juliana Gruenwald, Allan Shuldiner, September Trevino.
Line drawings: Talia Greenberg
Photographs: Reuters; Richard Ellis, 38, 131; Scott Ferrell, 78, 135; R. Michael Jenkins, 98; State of Tennessee, 33.
Cover design: Eloise Fuller

Library of Congress Cataloging-in-Publication Data

Candidates '96 : profiles of presidential contenders / Ronald D. Elving, editor.
     p.   cm.
     Includes index.
     ISBN 1-56802-217-4 (paper :   alk. paper)
     1. Presidents--United States--Election--1996.   2. Presidential candidates--United States.   3. United States--Politics and government--1993–   I. Congressional Quarterly Inc.
E888.C36   1995   95-45283
973.929'092'2--dc20

Contents

★　　★　　★

Preface

Candidates '96 is a handbook for students and citizens who want to follow the development of the presidential election campaign of 1996. Readers will find essays about the major candidates who were running in late 1995, as well as descriptions of many of the less prominent individuals who were seeking the office or somehow affecting the race. The portraits of the leading candidates include boxed material highlighting aspects of each individual's career and achievements, as well as synopses of important votes cast, voting analysis scores and interest group ratings for those who have served in Congress.

These essays were prepared by Congressional Quarterly's political staff, under the direction of political editor Ronald D. Elving, in the late spring through early fall of 1995. The essays should be read with that timeframe in mind, as a political campaign is by definition a moving target with important changes taking place from week to week. For example, as this book was being completed, retired Army general Colin Powell decided not to seek the presidency, thereby removing a major wildcard from the race. Soon after Powell's announcement, Arlen Specter, a Republican senator from Pennsylvania, suspended his campaign, in important part because of fundraising difficulties.

By the end of 1995 other candidates in the crowded Republican field may have dropped out. By late winter, when the plethora of primaries are history, the Republican field will be reduced to a small number and probably to a single all-but-nominated individual. But the candidates who do not succeed in the primaries will not necessarily become history themselves. Some may become candidates for the vice presidential slot on the GOP ticket. Others, both Republican and Democrat, may decide to enter the race as independents.

There also looms for 1996, as in 1992, a strong likelihood of a significant third-party presence involving the efforts of independent H. Ross Perot. The Perot and third-party phenomena are chronicled in a separate report in the book.

Candidates '96 begins with an introduction that analyzes the political terrain in the fall of 1995. The essay on President Clinton, the incumbent and only candidate for the Democratic nomination, appears first. This is followed by reports on the major Republican candidates, listed alphabetically. A description of the third-party movement, profiles of other candidates in the race and an appendix on how caucuses and primaries affect the presidential nominating process conclude the book.

Introduction

American elections are usually difficult to predict, at least until the final weeks, when the average voter focuses on the candidates and what separates them from each other. From a distance, no one can foretell the state of the economy and world affairs on Election Day, and no one can say with assurance which voters will feel most motivated to turn out.

Poll after poll finds the electorate disappointed with the new Democratic president it chose in 1992 and dismayed with some actions of the new Republican Congress it chose in 1994. The simplest way to settle the unstable politics of the moment would be to elect a president with a preponderant share of the vote that imparts a clear mandate to govern, but the system is as likely to produce an electoral result that does the opposite.

The 1996 election cycle is apt to be complicated by factors that have the potential to transform our expectations about presidential politics. November 1996 may bring not a two-way contest but a struggle between three or more candidates strong enough to influence the outcome. We may witness an unusual confluence of circumstances and personalities potent enough to overcome the two-party voting pattern so deeply ingrained in White House history.

Speculation had focused on retired Army general Colin L. Powell, the former chairman of the Joint Chiefs of Staff whose autobiography and book tour mesmerized the news media throughout the summer of 1995 and into the fall. Snatching back the headlines in September was Ross Perot, the mercurial Texas billionaire whose 1992 bid for the White House garnered roughly one vote in five. Powell removed himself from contention with his official announcement November 8 stating that he would not be a candidate for any elective office in 1996, but his impact had already been felt.

As different as these two men are from each other, their prospective candidacies had much in common. Each in his own way has traded on the idea that professional politicians should wield less power and that people from other walks of life should be encouraged to seek public office at all levels. Each also has drawn strength from the belief that the current leadership in both parties is both intellectually and ethically corrupt.

Perot, the wildly successful businessman, and Powell, the improbably successful career soldier, both embody the extraordinary individualism that appeals to voters. Their appeal lies in the vivid contrast they pose to longtime officeholders, who are perceived as unprincipled and self-serving in their intricate dealmaking —even if they are simply compromising for the sake of getting something done.

Clinton himself might have lent the current imbalance some equilibrium by being decidedly popular. Conversely, he might have tipped the scales by being thoroughly unpopular. But he is neither. His Gallup approval rating has rarely seen the sunny side of 50 since his early weeks in office (hyperactive and luckless as they were). The most he can hope for is to be re-elected in a close call, with his victory attributable either to the errors of the GOP or to the dynamics of a multiple-candidate field.

Polls show as many as three Americans in five (62 percent) would like to see a third party. Unlike years past, these sentiments are voiced not only by strong conservatives or dedicated liberals but also by lifelong occupants of the political middle. The same polls had shown Powell leading both President Bill Clinton and Sen. Bob Dole, R-Kan., in a three-way race. The last time anyone had been in such a position was nearly 44 years ago, when Gen. Dwight D. Eisenhower loomed over Democratic incumbent Harry S. Truman and his main GOP rival, Republican Sen. Robert A. Taft, en route to election as president in 1952.

Perot launched a third party of his own in September 1995, when Powell's plans were still unknown. Powell's remarkable standing attested to two factors affecting the future of American politics. One is that the dissatisfaction with Clinton has not led the public to embrace his Republican challengers, either individually or as a group. The other is that much of the public shares Powell's sense of separation from both of the major parties. Many voters, if not a majority, are less doctrinaire than the parties, which are increasingly dominated by their most orthodox constituencies. This would suggest that as voters look beyond the parties for political saviors, they may look beyond the parties for policy prescriptions as well.

The Clinton Chance

Clinton completed his thirty-third month in the White House with an approval rating just below 50 percent in most polls. Some measures found a roughly commensurate number (about 45 percent) willing to say they would not vote to re-elect Clinton under any circumstances. At base, Clinton's numbers had not changed appreciably since he ousted George Bush with just 43 percent of the total popular vote in November 1992.

In previous elections, such raw Gallup tallies have been poor predictors of the eventual outcome. Both Richard M. Nixon and Ronald Reagan were below 50 percent in the Gallup at a comparable point, yet each won re-election carrying 49 states. Each managed to reclaim his momentum in the re-election year and present a winning contrast to the opposition party's nominee (while keeping his distance from his own party's congressional candidates).

Clinton will be striving to emulate this strategy on all counts. If he is to succeed, it will be with the unwilling assistance of the Republican themselves. Having fulfilled a dream in 1994 by recapturing the majority not only in the Senate but also in the House for the first time in four decades, the GOP is marching with confidence that exceeds even the headiest days of Reagan's ascendancy.

By tackling the difficult issues of Medicare and Medicaid, and cutting back smaller programs popular with voters, the congressional Republicans have given Clinton a chance to recast himself as Horatius at the bridge—despite his own efforts to restrain spending in some of the same areas. By simultaneously pushing through large tax cuts, some of which benefit the wealthiest taxpayers, the GOP opens itself to populist counterattacks from the Democrats and allows Clinton to claim that his tax cuts are more moderate.

GOP Calculations

When Republicans think about presidential elections, they like to think about the tote board for the Electoral College. Based on the results of elections over the past 30 years, Republicans assume they will carry the South, the Plains and the Mountain West. Any kind of showing at all in the Northeast or on the West Coast should add up to an easy Electoral College triumph.

They also realize that Clinton might slip through in enough states to amass the 270 electoral votes needed for re-election. They are uneasy because, while the party line says any Republican will beat Clinton, the private fear is that Dole or one of his rivals could come up short. Unease about this field contributes both to Clinton's renewed confidence and to the surging interest in non-Republican alternatives.

The GOP Field

With the first delegate-selecting events months away, Dole was under full sail—a single tall ship surrounded by a squadron of lesser vessels. He had raised the most money, amassed the most endorsements and enjoyed a more than two-to-one lead in the polls over his nearest opponent. In this, his third and by far his best-organized and best-financed run for president, he had acceded to the kind of front-runner status that usually leads to the nomination (especially in the hierarchical confines of the Republican Party).

While age and experience are often assets, Dole may have a little too much of both for his own good. If elected, he would be 73 when inaugurated, making him the oldest new president in U.S. history. Having had 40 years in elective office, 26 in the Senate, he had a hard time connecting with the new Republican activists' enthusiasm for citizen legislators. Like all front-runners, Dole was easily victimized by the slightest ill luck, as his disappointing showing in the largely meaningless Iowa straw poll in August demonstrated. In short, Dole reigned in 1995 as a kind of glass-jaw champion, the beneficiary of broad but shallow support based more on familiarity than on strong voter affinity.

His nearest competitor in the polls, aside from Powell, was his colleague and rival in the Senate, Phil Gramm of Texas, the hard-charging former Democrat who moved the Gramm-Rudman law through Congress in his first year as a senator. As chairman of the GOP Senate campaign committee since 1991, Gramm had lead the money chase in the early months of 1995 and logged many miles helping other Republicans raise money and win elections. He was more consistent in his views than Dole, compiling a rating of 96 from the American Conservative Union during his decade in the Senate (Dole's was 89 over the same period) and trying harder to corner the votes of social activists.

Running third by most measures was Patrick J. Buchanan, a former speechwriter for both Reagan and Nixon who took on President Bush in the primaries in 1992. While he hobbled the president for the course of the campaign, Buchanan never won a primary or state caucus that year. That is one reason his current effort has been comparatively underfunded.

Buchanan connects with audiences with a blend of populism and nationalism, and he can blister his rhetorical targets as well as anyone. He has the endorsement of the influential *Manchester Union-Leader* in New Hampshire and could prove to be Dole's main conservative rival in that state.

If Dole should stumble, his role as establishment choice might be taken by someone from the third tier of Republican aspirants, which includes Sen. Richard Lugar of Indiana and former governor Lamar Alexander of Tennessee. In the autumn of 1995, both were in single digits in the polls, and neither showed any sign of breaking out. Both presented attractive profiles as running mates, and either could catch fire if a true vacuum were to develop at the center.

Another prospect of uncertain promise was Malcolm S. "Steve" Forbes Jr., scion of the Forbes publishing empire, who said he would spend up to $25 million of his own money to promote his message of tax cuts as a stimulant to economic growth. Forbes' candidacy grew out of frustration with the existing field, which he said failed to capture the upbeat spirit of former president Ronald Reagan.

The rest of the field consisted of candidates pursuing the nomination primarily to gain exposure for their careers or their causes. Sen. Arlen Specter of Pennsylvania, whose longshot bid never took off, campaigned as a centrist within the party. By supporting abortion rights, he earned the enmity of most party activists. His inability to raise funds forced his withdrawal from the race. Rep. Robert K.

Dornan of California and former State Department official Alan Keyes, a talk show host and two-time Senate candidate in Maryland, were emphasizing their antiabortion stands. Businessman Maurice Taylor, who like Forbes volunteered to bankroll his own effort, was playing up his credentials as an outsider and a nonpolitician.

Gov. Pete Wilson of California, one of the last Republicans to enter the race, was the first to exit, announcing September 29 that he could not raise enough money to continue.

House Speaker Newt Gingrich, R-Ga., who led the Republican revolution in the House, announced in November that he would not seek the nomination.

Looking Ahead

As 1995 comes to a close, little has been settled about the Republican or general election field. Even if candidates do not enter the primaries, they can seek an independent line on the ballot state by state. This was the route taken by Ross Perot in 1992, when his 19-percent share of the vote was the best showing for a third-option candidate since Theodore Roosevelt ran in 1912.

Perot may still run again in 1996, and the list of potential independents who wish to join the fray has been unusually long and interesting. Civil rights activist Jesse Jackson, unwilling to take on Clinton in the primaries, has spoken of an independent bid in the fall. Announcing his retirement from the Senate in August, Sen. Bill Bradley, D-N.J., said he would think about running outside his party. Expressing similar thoughts was former Republican Sen. Lowell P. Weicker Jr. of Connecticut, one of two New England governors to be elected as independents in the 1990s.

Conventional wisdom has long held that independent or third-party candidates for president never win; they throw the election to one of the two major parties. However, the 1990s have not been hospitable to conventional wisdom. The surprises of 1992 and 1994 may be trumped by an even more dramatic breakthrough in 1996.

Ronald D. Elving
November 1995

Leading Candidates

Bill Clinton

Bill Clinton is gearing up to seek a prize that only one of the last four occupants of the White House has achieved: re-election. No Democrat has been elected president and then re-elected to a second full term since Franklin D. Roosevelt more than half a century ago.

By conventional standards, Clinton's prospects of overcoming these historical odds would seem poor. His party lost control of both chambers of Congress in the 1994 midterm elections, a debacle for which many Democrats hold him responsible. Clinton's presidency has never gained much altitude, nor has his base significantly expanded beyond the 43 percent of the vote he won in 1992.

While the economy has flourished by most measures, Clinton has received little credit. His management of foreign relations has flirted with disaster in Somalia, the Caribbean, the Balkans and the Far East. He has been hounded by allegations both legal and personal that stem from his years as governor of Arkansas.

Clinton's presidential approval rating in the Gallup Poll has never reached 60 percent, a standard that most presidents easily surpass during the traditional "honeymoon" of their first months in office. Clinton has spent much of his term mired below 50 percent. His Gallup approval rating in late August stood at 46 percent, roughly where it had been over the past year and not much different from the 43 percent share of the vote he received in 1992.

Yet even his most partisan adversaries on Capitol Hill are loath to write him off. "He has a very realistic opportunity to get re-elected," said House Speaker Newt Gingrich, R-Ga., in September. Few politicians of any stripe were saying that at the end of 1994. After

Bill Clinton

Democrat of Little Rock, Ark.
Born: Aug. 19, 1946; Hope, Ark.
Education: Georgetown University, B.S.F.S.,
 1968; Rhodes scholar, Oxford University,
 1968–70; Yale Law School, J.D. 1973.
Family: Wife, Hillary Rodham Clinton; one
 child, Chelsea.
Religion: Baptist.
Political career: Nominee for U.S. House,
 1974; state attorney general, 1977–79; governor, 1979–81; nominee for governor, 1980; governor, 1983–93;
president, 1993–
Professional career: Law professor, University of Arkansas, 1973–76.

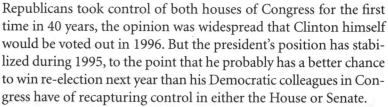

Republicans took control of both houses of Congress for the first time in 40 years, the opinion was widespread that Clinton himself would be voted out in 1996. But the president's position has stabilized during 1995, to the point that he probably has a better chance to win re-election next year than his Democratic colleagues in Congress have of recapturing control in either the House or Senate.

Clinton has benefited from a shifting of the spotlight. Attention has turned from his rocky relationship with the Democratic-controlled 103rd Congress to the controversial initiatives of the Republican 104th Congress, with its social conservatism and budget-cutting zeal. As the new majority tackles its agenda, it takes risks before a skeptical public. Some recent polling shows trust in the new Congress declining as apprehension over its direction grows. A Gallup measure in August for CNN and *USA Today* found only 30 percent of respondents approved of the way Congress was handling its job.

This focus on Congress has enabled Clinton to appear more centrist than he ever did during his first two years in office. And the thematic underpinnings of a re-election campaign have become visible. Georgetown University political scientist Stephen Wayne says Clinton is less apt to run on his own record than as a safer alternative to the GOP agenda and whomever it nominates against him. In this role, said Wayne, Clinton would portray himself as "a mainstreamer . . . a non-ideologue . . . a moderate."

Up from the Depths

Clinton's political fortunes struck a low point with his party's devastating losses in the 1994 elections. Republicans made the midterm a referendum on Clinton, airing television ads in which a given Democratic candidate's face was slowly transformed into Clinton's.

"After some months of shock and floundering, I think the president has found his sea legs in this new environment," said Thomas E. Mann, director of governmental studies at the Brookings Institution.

Rep. Sherwood Boehlert, a moderate Republican from New York, however, said he believes "the jury is still out" on how Clinton has related to the new order in Congress and on Clinton's own prospects for re-election.

In many ways, Clinton's chances for re-election may have improved under a GOP-led Congress, some Democrats and observers say. If Democrats had remained in control with a reduced majority, Clinton might still have been expected to produce on his agenda. But with Republicans running Congress, Mann argued, Clinton may now be judged on his ability "to control the Republican extremism and channel it in a constructive way."

In addition, Clinton now has something to run against from the outset of the 1996 cycle. After searching for a strategy, he has moved into painting the GOP as having gone too far in their efforts to reduce government spending and slim down the federal bureaucracy.

"The president's fortunes are improving daily; I think in large part because . . . the Republican House and Senate is making it easier for the president to define and differentiate his policies from those of the Republican led-Congress," said Rep. Cal Dooley, a three-term conservative Democrat from California. Dooley and other Clinton supporters say the president is re-establishing himself as the centrist they knew in 1992.

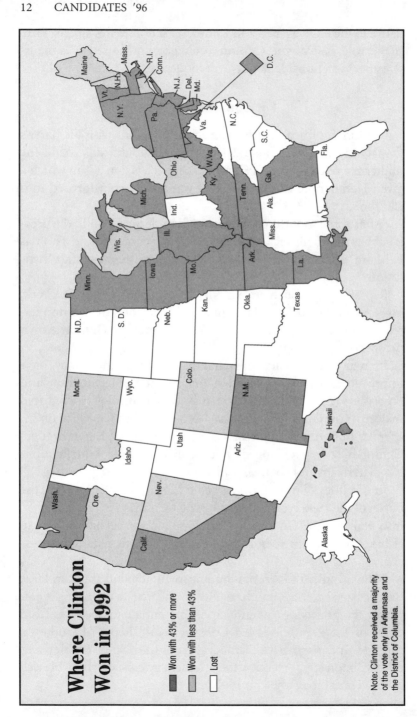

Where Clinton Won in 1992

■ Won with 43% or more

▨ Won with less than 43%

□ Lost

Note: Clinton received a majority of the vote only in Arkansas and the District of Columbia.

Clinton can, for example, present a more gradual approach to Medicare cost-cutting than the GOP proposal to cut $270 billion over seven years. "I think the Medicare debate will have a big effect on (Clinton's) re-election," said Sen. Tom Harkin, D-Iowa. "I think a lot of elderly people who vote are going to be upset when they see exactly what the GOP plans to do."

Clinton appears to be betting that the public will reward him for restraining an overzealous GOP. "He's going to be able to say that he stopped the extremism of the right-wing Republicans . . . that he kept the country from moving too far to the right and off the cliff," said Rep. Robert T. Matsui, D-Calif.

Even Republicans acknowledge that Clinton is a likable, engaging campaigner. For the moment, at least, he can point to a comparatively peaceful stasis in world affairs and a stream of good news on the economic front. Not only have the financial markets enjoyed a banner year, but the economy as a whole has shown sustainable growth with low inflation and low unemployment.

Ron Walters, a Howard University political scientist, foresees the president saying that "the first two years he got things done [and] the second two years he prevented things from being done that would hurt you." Walters notes that, "where possible, [Clinton would say he] compromised with Republicans to get bipartisan legislation." But he expects it to be even more important for Clinton to have resisted the new congressional majority.

In the end, Walters says, Clinton's own record will be less important than what voters feel about the actions of the GOP Congress. "The only thing keeping him afloat," said Walters, is the prospect that "Americans will perceive the Republicans have gone too far."

Taking Both Sides

But finding this footing has been a slow and painful struggle. The Republican victory caught the White House off guard, and it showed in Clinton's reaction to the Contract with America and its balanced-budget amendment, tax cuts and term limits.

"Republicans were very certain about what the election meant and the president was uncertain about what the election meant," said Richard F. Fenno, a political scientist at the University of

Wins Did More to Fuel Critics' Fires . . .

When President Clinton presents his record to voters in 1996, much of the legislative agenda he fought for in the 103rd Congress will have been superseded by the battles of the 104th.

His record from the 103rd ranges from the narrow passage of the massive budget-reconciliation bill in 1993 to the collapse of a comprehensive health care reform package in 1994.

He pressed for a tax increase on higher incomes and gasoline, as well as for tighter restrictions on handguns and assault weapons. Both issues galvanized opposition far more than a declining budget deficit and healthy economic growth stimulated support.

Clinton stumbled early in 1993 over his choice for attorney general, Zoë Baird, who admitted hiring undoc-

Clinton signs the Brady Bill as former White House press secretary James Brady, the bill's namesake, looks on.

umented aliens to care for her child, and his plan to lift the ban on homosexuals in the military. On both issues, Clinton was forced to back down.

The first substantive bill Clinton signed, in February 1993, was the Family and Medical Leave Act, which required employers to give unpaid leave to workers with newborn children or other pressing circumstances. The bill had been passed in nearly identical form in the previous Congress and required little more than Clinton's signature.

Two months later, the first piece of his economic plan, a $16.3 billion economic stimulus package, was killed in the Senate by Republican opposition and lukewarm Democratic support.

The biggest battle and greatest success of his administration came in August with the passage of the deficit-reducing budget reconciliation bill of 1993. As passed, the bill was expected to cut the deficit by $496 billion over five years through a mix of tax increases and budget cuts. While the bill's tax increases fell primarily on the wealthiest taxpayers,

... Than to Help President's Ratings

Republicans characterized the bill as a burden on all income brackets and attacked it as "the biggest tax increase in history." Several Democrats who voted for the bill were defeated for re-election in 1994.

Clinton's first major success on trade was the passage in November of the North American Free Trade Agreement (NAFTA). Clinton had to turn to the House Republicans, led by GOP Whip Newt Gingrich of Georgia, to find the votes essential for passage.

A few days after NAFTA was adopted, the Clinton administration chalked up another win when the Senate cleared the Brady Bill, a measure requiring a five-day waiting period for the purchase of a handgun.

Other successes in the 1993 session included passage of the "motor voter" law, which eased voter registration by linking it to the driver's license process. Clinton also got his Americorps program by which college grants could be earned through community service.

After his shaky start, Clinton was perceived as having found his footing as the 1993 legislative session ended. The second session would prove acutely disappointing.

In March, Congress approved the administration's Goals 2000 program, a measure that established national education goals for the country's schools. From then on, Clinton's fortunes steadily declined.

His top legislative priority—a sweeping plan to restructure the nation's health care system—died in September. The plan divided Democrats, who could not agree on the contents of the bill, and generally united Republicans.

Clinton eked out a victory on the $30.2 billion crime bill. It included the ban on assault weapons, as well as funding for prevention programs, prison construction and additional police officers. Once again, Clinton had to deal with Gingrich and his troops, reshaping the bill to gain their votes.

Unified behind the Contract with America theme, Republicans closed ranks in the fall weeks to frustrate Democratic efforts on campaign finance, lobbying disclosure, telecommunications and toxic waste.

The only other major piece of legislation enacted with administration backing in the 103rd was a bill implementing a renewal of the General Agreement on Tariffs and Trade. This victory, however, came during a lame duck session following the Democrats' devastating losses in November.

Rochester. "That uncertainty has been underlying in his behavior since."

The best Clinton could do in the first blush of Republican success was to adopt a "me too" attitude, said Martha Phillips, executive director of the Concord Coalition, an anti-deficit lobbying group. "He was bidding for a position in the game the Republicans had organized," Phillips said.

Five weeks after the 1994 elections, Clinton jumped on the tax cut bandwagon with his own proposal for $60 billion worth of tax cuts over five years targeted primarily at middle-income earners.

When Gingrich began promising a vote on a school prayer amendment in the GOP-led 104th Congress, Clinton offered some positive comments on the issue. He later said he opposed a constitutional amendment and favored clarifying what was already permissible under the Constitution.

In June, he offered his own 10-year balanced budget, which included cuts in Medicare and taxes, as a substitute to the budget he had proposed in February (and which had been almost totally ignored). Mann and some Democrats say the 10-year budget was a good move because it has provided Clinton with an alternative to contrast with Republican cuts he says go too deep. It angered some congressional Democrats at the time, who saw it as an embarrassing reversal of their line, voiced by Clinton as well, that a balanced budget with tax cuts was a bad mix.

After that, Clinton joined congressional Democrats in attacking a number of the majority's spending bills. Clinton vetoed several of the 13 appropriations bills, as well as the reconciliation legislation that enforces long-term decisions made earlier in the budget resolution (H Rept 104-159).

Clinton has criticized Republicans for making deep cuts in some of the bills in such areas as education and health and adding provisions, as the House did, that would limit the Environmental Protection Agency from enforcing a variety of anti-pollution laws. GOP appropriators also took aim at two of Clinton's most cherished programs by approving spending bills in the House that kill funding for the National Service initiative and Goals 2000 education reform program (the Senate has agreed to stop funding National Service).

Veto Total: Three

Clinton cast his third veto Oct. 3, making good a threat made months earlier against the legislative appropriations bill that funds Congress and its support agencies. Clinton did not quarrel with the bill itself but said Congress should not be taking care of its own funding ahead of the other appropriations categories.

In his first 33 months in office, Clinton had vetoed just two bills, both in the summer of 1995. The first veto forced Republicans to scale back somewhat on the amount of 1995 spending they wanted to rescind in midyear. The second preserved U.S. cooperation with the international arms embargo on the Muslim-led government of Bosnia.

In vetoing the rescissions bill, Clinton cited specific cuts and also the language that would accelerate certain timber sales in national forests. But in the end he angered some of his strongest supporters in the environmental movement by signing a modified bill that restored some funding and essentially left the controversial timber language intact.

Clinton also has threatened a veto over the size of the Medicare cuts proposed by the GOP. Republicans claim that the double-digit growth of Medicare and Medicaid, which the GOP has proposed cutting by $182 billion over seven years, will bankrupt the government. The GOP has proposed putting its Medicare and Medicaid plans in the budget-reconciliation bill.

Clinton, who himself proposed cutting Medicare by $128 billion and Medicaid by $54 billion in his 10-year budget plan, says the GOP's proposal is too extreme and is being manufactured to pay for tax cuts for the wealthy. Medicare provides health care coverage for senior citizens and Medicaid offers basic health care for the poor and disabled.

"This is not what it takes to save Medicare," Clinton said Sept. 15. "If these health care cuts come to my desk, of this size, I would have no choice but to veto it."

David M. Mason, a political analyst from the conservative think tank the Heritage Foundation, said Clinton has already given up ground by offering Medicare cuts of his own. "This is not the issue that will get him re-elected," Mason said. He added, however, that

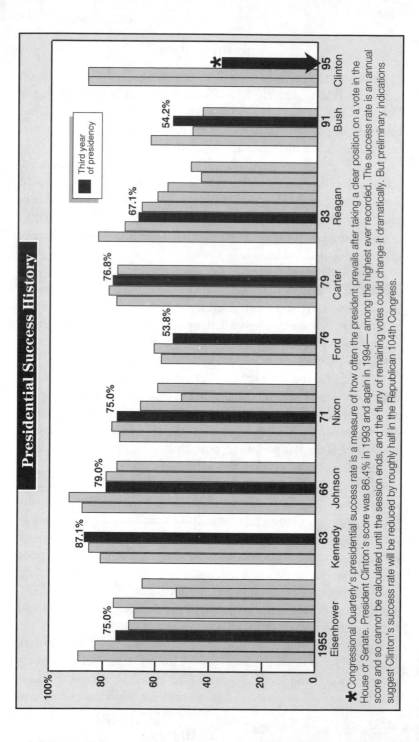

Presidential Success History

★ Congressional Quarterly's presidential success rate is a measure of how often the president prevails after taking a clear position on a vote in the House or Senate. President Clinton's score was 86.4% in 1993 and again in 1994— among the highest ever recorded. The success rate is an annual score and so cannot be calculated until the session ends, and the flurry of remaining votes could change it dramatically. But preliminary indications suggest Clinton's success rate will be reduced by roughly half in the Republican 104th Congress.

Legend: ■ Third year of presidency

X-axis labels: 1955 Eisenhower | 63 Kennedy | 66 Johnson | 71 Nixon | 76 Ford | 79 Carter | 83 Reagan | 91 Bush | 95 Clinton

Data labels: 75.0% (Eisenhower), 87.1% (Kennedy), 79.0% (Johnson), 75.0% (Nixon), 53.8% (Ford), 76.8% (Carter), 67.1% (Reagan), 54.2% (Bush)

the overall budget battle provides Clinton with an opportunity to improve his standing. "It will come to how deft of a politician he can be [in withstanding] what will be a substantive defeat."

Too Many Maneuvers?

Clinton critics are often wary of counting him out because he has shown a knack for finding his way back in. But with this facility the incumbent president risks appearing unprincipled.

When Clinton completed a policy review regarding affirmative action in July 1995 by announcing support for such programs, he received as much applause for having taken a foursquare position as for the position he took.

"There is a lack of consistency in terms of themes and action," said Boehlert, echoing a criticism heard from members of both parties on issues from the budget to foreign policy.

After Clinton offered his 10-year plan to balance the budget, Wisconsin Rep. David R. Obey, the ranking Democrat on the House Appropriations Committee, said: "Most of us learned some time ago that if you don't like the president's position on a particular issue, you simply need to wait a few weeks."

On foreign policy, Clinton's actions to achieve peace in Bosnia-Herzegovina have been criticized as indecisive and ineffective. Congress approved legislation in August to require the president to unilaterally lift the international arms embargo against the Bosnian government, leading to Clinton's second veto. In the late summer, Clinton appeared to turn a corner on this issue after the United States and its NATO allies launched a bombing campaign that seemed to force the defiant Bosnian Serbs to withdraw some of their heavy weapons from the siege of Sarajevo.

In addition, Clinton has had some measure of success in advancing peace negotiations in Northern Ireland and, most notably, in the Middle East. An agreement providing for greater Palestinian control of the West Bank was signed Sept. 28 under his aegis in Washington. Given these successes, voter irritation with Clinton's perceived lack of focus seems to be muted. He "goes about four ways at once," said Lawrence Longley, a Lawrence University, Wisconsin, political scientist and a member of the Democratic National Committee. But that, Longley adds, may be an effective contrast to a conservative-led, litmus-test-oriented GOP. "He is diffuse and that may be his strength in 1996."

Mann said Clinton has been using powers at his disposal, such as issuing executive orders and taking a more aggressive stance as a foreign policy leader. "He's acting more and more like a president," he said.

Underlying Weakness

If the political breezes of the autumn seem friendlier to the president, it is by no means clear that his storms are behind him. He has been bedeviled by questions about his personal character since the early stages of his 1992 presidential campaign. The Whitewater real estate affair has produced criminal indictments against some of his former associates in Arkansas, and investigations continue. A potentially embarrassing court proceeding on charges of sexual harassment also hovers on the horizon.

If Clinton has benefited in some respects from the Republican management of Congress in 1995, he is still suffering politically for what happened during the last two years of Democratic control. Any list of the memorable events from that period would include Clinton's effort to permit gays to serve openly in the military, his push for tax increases and his failure to move his overhaul of the health-care system even close to enactment.

To the extent that he has come back, said Emory University political scientist Merle Black, he has "played off his opponents, not [shown] inherent strength of his own."

The Electoral Problem

It must also be remembered that presidential elections are not conducted by poll, and the winner is not elected by the popular vote. What is essential is a majority in the Electoral College, and this challenge at times looks all the more daunting for Clinton.

When looking at the current electoral vote map, it is far easier to see how Republicans reach the 270 votes needed for victory than Clinton. Republicans enjoy a long head start in most of the South,

No Shortage of Scrutiny

Few presidents have survived as much scandal as Bill Clinton had survived before he even reached the White House. While 1995 brought no new stories to sully Clinton's personal reputation, investigations that began earlier continued to burden his administration.

On Oct. 2, Sen. Alfonse M. D'Amato, R-N.Y., announced that the Senate Banking Committee would resume its probe of the Whitewater real estate venture, which involved both Clinton and his wife, Hillary, while Clinton was governor of Arkansas.

Whitewater is also the subject of an investigation by special federal prosecutor Kenneth W. Starr, who has already obtained grand jury indictments of several Arkansas figures with Clinton ties (including Clinton's successor as governor, Democrat Jim Guy Tucker).

The House Banking Committee, led by Chairman Jim Leach, R-Iowa, is also looking into Whitewater.

Earlier in the summer, D'Amato held two weeks of hearings inquiring into the Whitewater implications of the suicide of Vincent W. Foster. A former law partner of Mrs. Clinton, Foster came to Washington in 1993 to serve as deputy White House counsel. Foster's death has been ruled a suicide by law enforcement agencies and by the first special prosecutor tapped to investigate. It remains a source of fascination for many.

Affairs Alleged

Even before the first primary of 1992, Clinton was accused of having had a long-term affair with a nightclub singer in Little Rock during his governorship. The singer, Gennifer Flowers, sold her story to supermarket tabloids and TV gossip shows, forcing the Clintons to submit to long broadcast interviews on the subject.

Another woman, Paula Jones, filed a lawsuit in 1994 charging that she had been sexually harassed by Clinton when he was governor of Arkansas. In December 1994 a federal court granted a stay in the Jones matter, accepting the White House contention that the president should not be subject to civil suits while in office. That ruling has been appealed.

The Clinton administration has also been bruised by investigations into the behavior of the FBI and the Bureau of Alcohol, Tobacco and Firearms at the Branch Davidian compound near Waco, Texas, and at the Ruby Ridge, Idaho, cabin of Randy Weaver.

Clinton's Campaign in 1996 . . .

President Clinton has been casting a wide net as he assembles a political team for his 1996 re-election bid.

Among those already on board, the most controversial is political consultant Richard Morris, who is best known for such high-profile Republican clients as Senate Majority Whip Trent Lott of Mississippi. Morris has been advising the president on policy issues and has helped craft a more centrist message for Clinton.

Still, Morris's presence at the White House has created a stir. One Democratic political consultant described Morris as the "flavor of the month" who could fall out of favor with Clinton.

Hillary Clinton

Changes in the Cast

Several of the better known players from Clinton's 1992 campaign are unlikely to reprise their roles. One key consultant, Paul Begala, is already out of the mix. It remains unclear what role James Carville, Begala's former partner and Clinton's top political strategist in 1992, will have in Clinton's campaign team. Carville reportedly has had differences with Morris.

Stephanopoulos

Clinton's chief pollster in 1992, Stanley Greenberg, is also unlikely to be as prominent. Doug Schoen of the Democratic polling firm Penn & Schoen is said to be favored by Morris and is expected to be the campaign's top pollster.

Another 1992 veteran now in the background is media consultant Mandy Grunwald. Democratic consultant Bob Squier is expected to be among Clinton's leading media advisers.

Within the White House proper, Deputy Chief of Staff Harold Ickes is the lead political tactician. The in-house political staff includes operatives such as political affairs director Doug Sosnik, a former political

... Who's In and Who's Out

director at the Democratic Congressional Campaign Committee, and Craig Smith, who opened Clinton's first presidential campaign headquarters in Little Rock, Arkansas, in 1991.

Gore

Some of the political operatives, such as senior adviser George Stephanopoulos, who moved into governmental roles with Clinton after the 1992 election, may move back into campaign mode.

At the Top

Clinton will continue to be advised by his wife, Hillary, and by Vice President Al Gore. Gore has already weighed in on the 1996 campaign, hitting the road in recent months to urge the president's re-election in highly partisan tones. In September, he went to Iowa, site of the nation's first major delegate-selecting event of the nominating season, telling Democratic activists that the GOP's extreme and narrow message will work to the president's advantage. At a recent appearance before a labor union convention in Chicago, Gore pitched the same message, describing the Republican congressional leadership as "right-wing extremists."

Ickes

The first lady, however, has been far less vocal and visible in 1995 than she had been previously. She became a lightning rod for criticism during the 103rd Congress, when some critics held her responsible for her husband's perceived shift to the left. She also directed the writing of the health care overhaul plan, which later collapsed in Congress.

Since the Democratic debacle in the midterm elections of 1994, Mrs. Clinton has performed as a more traditional president's wife. All the same, the first lady will remain influential.

the Plains states and the Rocky Mountain West. George Bush won much of this territory in 1992 and GOP presidential candidates have dominated it over the last quarter-century.

If that remains the case again next year, then Clinton would need to draw to an inside straight in the rest of the country—the Northeast, the industrial Midwest and the Pacific West. "Democrats are back to an 18-to-20 state Electoral College strategy," said Wayne.

Clinton benefited from the independent candidacy of Ross Perot in 1992, whose supporters were disproportionately Republican-leaning. With Perot taking nearly one-fifth of the popular vote, Clinton was able to win the White House with just 43 percent, the fourth-lowest winning percentage in American history.

Perot now wants to start a third party, which presumably would be interested in nominating Perot. This is widely viewed as foreshadowing a replay of 1992. A *Los Angeles Times* poll taken in mid-September showed Clinton with 43 percent to 35 percent for Senate Majority Leader Bob Dole, R-Kan., and 20 percent for Perot. In 1992, Clinton got 43 percent of the vote to 37 percent for President George Bush and 19 percent for Perot.

Clinton cannot count on prospective independent candidates in 1996 to be as helpful. Running as an independent, Jesse Jackson would surely cut into the Democrats' traditional base among racial minorities. Sen. Bill Bradley, D-N.J., would presumably carve into other parts of the Democratic coalition.

Weakened Institution

Not long ago, the powers of the presidency and the respect attending them were so great that voters almost automatically gave Oval Office occupants a second term in office. From Franklin D. Roosevelt in 1936 to Richard M. Nixon in 1972, presidents were not only re-elected but rewarded with decisive margins. Presidential victories ranged from a comfortable 4.5 percentage points for Harry S. Truman in his come-from-behind win in 1948, to landslide triumphs of at least 15 percentage points for FDR in 1936, Dwight D. Eisenhower in 1956, Lyndon B. Johnson in 1964 and Nixon in 1972.

But Clinton must seek re-election in a more demanding era. In

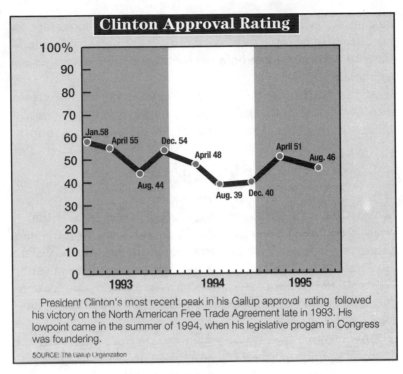

Clinton Approval Rating

President Clinton's most recent peak in his Gallup approval rating followed his victory on the North American Free Trade Agreement late in 1993. His lowpoint came in the summer of 1994, when his legislative progam in Congress was foundering.

SOURCE: The Gallup Organization

the last 20 years, Ronald Reagan has been the only president to win re-election. The others—Gerald R. Ford, Carter and Bush—all lost re-election bids. They made history in the process. Never before have so many presidents suffered rejection at the ballot box in so short a period of time.

For a time in early 1995, Clinton looked as though he would draw a primary challenge from former Pennsylvania governor Robert P. Casey, an outspoken foe of abortion. Casey ended his nascent campaign in April, citing health reasons.

That has left Clinton, at least for the time being, without opposition for renomination, just as Reagan was when he ran for re-election in 1984. Clinton has been quickly raising millions of campaign dollars to increase his likelihood of remaining unopposed. The president's campaign committee is expected to raise more than $25 million in 1995.

The absence of an intraparty challenge also has freed Clinton to focus on convincing voters that no matter what their doubts about him, he is growing into the role of president. The Clinton campaign has already done some spot advertising in potential battleground states such as Colorado promoting the administration's anti-crime legislation.

At the same time, the crowded Republican race has grown increasingly contentious. An array of national polls have shown Clinton moving well ahead of Dole, the Republican front-runner.

Firming Up the Base

The assertive nature of the Republican Congress seems to have helped Clinton solidify support within the Democratic coalition. A clear majority of liberals, minorities and low-income voters approved of Clinton's job performance in the late August Gallup approval ratings. Clinton also drew majority support from young voters (18 to 29 years old), self-described moderates, and Easterners (the regional building block for Democrats in fashioning Electoral College majorities).

On the discouraging side, Clinton's performance won the approval of only one-third of Perot voters, roughly the same percentage that backed Democratic congressional candidates during the party's disastrous showing at the ballot box in 1994.

From his vantage point in Ohio, University of Akron political scientist John C. Green sees many voters taking a "wait and see attitude" toward both Clinton and the Republican Congress. "They kicked out George Bush and they kicked out the Democratic Congress," says Green. The feeling for now is "let's give [both of] them a little room."

That mood could change quickly in the weeks ahead. The fall before a presidential election year is often when trend lines are established for the year to come.

"It was in the fourth quarter of 1991," writes Lydia Saad, managing editor of the Gallup Poll, "that George Bush's ratings tumbled 16 points, ending his Gulf War bonanza, after which he descended sharply, and permanently, below 50 percent. Conversely, it was in this quarter of 1983 that Ronald Reagan broke out of a seven-quarter slump and reached approval levels above 50 percent, which he then maintained throughout the election campaign."

Reagan was boosted by an economy rapidly recovering from recession; Bush was burdened by the perception of an economy sinking into recession.

While the state of the economy is a staple of politics, far more than pocketbook concerns will be affecting voter opinions of Clinton in the months ahead, as the Democrats at one end of Pennsylvania Avenue and the Republicans at the other struggle to define the role of government.

"At this point," said Stephen Hess of the Brookings Institution, "I wouldn't bet on him but I would not necessarily bet against him. It's a crazy year."

Lamar Alexander

L amar Alexander has built a reputation in politics as a good sales-man. As Tennessee's governor, the Republican helped persuade both Nissan Motor Co. and General Motors to build an auto plant in his state.

He successfully fought the Tennessee Education Association and persuaded the state legislature to pass an education reform program that included merit pay for teachers. He also prevailed on legislators to pass higher gas and sales taxes to pay for better roads and schools.

But Alexander now has thrust himself into the biggest sales competition of all—a presidential nominating campaign—with the goal of selling himself to an ascendant Republican Party as its strongest champion in 1996.

Preference polls taken among Republican primary voters show most of those surveyed are not buying Alexander—at least not yet. Polls have shown him mired in single digits while the undisputed Republican front-runner, Senate Majority Leader Bob Dole of Kansas, remains the choice of roughly half the party.

Coming from back in the pack may be a tradition among Democrats, but Republicans tend to nominate the early leader or, once in a while, the early No. 2. Not since Wendell Willkie in 1940 has the GOP nominee started from as far back as Alexander does now.

Complicating the picture for the former two-term governor and secretary of education are three other factors: the election in 1994 of a Republican Congress, lingering questions about his own path to personal wealth and a nagging suspicion among party conservatives that he is not one of them.

Lamar Alexander

Republican of Nashville, Tenn.

Born: July 3, 1940; Maryville, Tenn.

Education: Vanderbilt University, B.A. 1962; New York University, J.D. 1965.

Family: Wife, Leslee "Honey" Buhler; four children: Andrew, Leslee, Kathryn and William.

Religion: Presbyterian.

Political career: 1974 Republican nominee for Tennessee governor; Tennessee governor, 1979–87.

Professional career: Law clerk, Judge John Minor Wisdom, 5th U.S. Circuit Court of Appeals, 1965–66; legislative assistant, Sen. Howard H. Baker Jr. 1967–68; executive assistant, White House Congressional Liaison Office, 1969–70; founding partner, Dearborn and Ewing law firm, 1970–76; campaign manager, Republican gubernatorial candidate Winfield Dunn, 1970; chairman, Leadership Institute at Belmont University, 1987–88; president, University of Tennessee, 1988–91; U.S. secretary of education, 1991–93; counsel, Baker, Donelson, Bearman & Caldwell law firm, 1993–95.

Alexander began his presidential explorations in 1994, sounding one theme above all others: an attack on members of Congress and a call to "cut their pay and send them home." Alexander said Congress should meet only six months a year and be paid only half of the $133,600 that members are paid now.

Alexander said he still supports the idea of a part-time Congress, but he has muted his criticism in the wake of his party's triumph.

More nettlesome are the issues raised by several inquiries into Alexander's financial success, beginning with the Senate confirmation hearings prior to his joining President George Bush's Cabinet in 1991.

Alexander's appeal to conservatives, a dominant force within the primary electorate of the party Ronald Reagan built, was based in part on his hostility to Congress. Now he must find new ways to market a political record that is short on red-meat appeal for the right.

As governor, he was not known as a tax hawk, and he has taken a finessed, middle-of-the-road position on abortion, an issue he was not forced to deal with.

Still, Alexander, 55, cannot be dismissed from discussions of the national ticket in 1996 and beyond. He has managed to attract six former finance chairmen of the Republican National Committee to his corner early, and they have helped him raise more than $8 million of the $20 million that many analysts say is needed to compete in the 1996 presidential primaries.

In fact, Alexander's smooth-functioning money machine would be the talk of any previous election cycle. In this race, however, Dole and Sen. Phil Gramm of Texas claim to have raised $19 million and $18.9 million, respectively.

But fundraising is not Alexander's only asset. During two terms as governor of Tennessee, he built a reputation for tenacity.

"One should never underestimate Lamar," said one longtime Tennessee political analyst. "He's very focused, very disciplined."

These are traits he learned and honed early as a musician gifted and accomplished enough that, after being elected governor, he often performed with Tennessee symphonies and orchestras to raise money. When he was younger, serving as a law clerk from 1965 to 1966 for Judge John Minor Wisdom of the 5th U.S. Circuit Court of Appeals, Alexander moonlighted as a musician in New Orleans nightclubs, playing the piano, trombone, even the washboard.

Natural Salesman

Alexander has learned the craft of appealing to people at their level. In this latest quest, he understands the dismay many voters have with Washington and so has cast himself as a folksy outsider. He has been campaigning on returning governmental power to the state and local levels. "We are not too stupid to know what to do," he often says.

In preparation for his presidential bid, Alexander spent two months of the summer of 1994 driving across the country gathering ideas and advice.

Alexander's Highlights as . . .

During eight years (1979–87) as Tennessee governor, Republican Lamar Alexander's greatest challenge was his educational reform effort, known as the Better Schools Program. The $1.2 billion program's centerpiece was a merit pay plan for teachers. Other aspects of the 10-point plan included establishing basic skills and computer skills programs, establishing a summer program for gifted children and hiring more math and science teachers.

Alexander proposed paying for the plan largely with a 1-cent increase in the state sales tax. The plan was defeated when he first introduced it in 1983, in large part because of opposition from the teachers union, which staunchly opposed the "career ladder" merit pay provision that called for allowing teachers to earn more money if they did well on performance evaluations.

Selling to the Public

After its defeat, he embarked on a sales campaign across the state for his education plan. In the final weeks of the negotiations in early 1984, Alexander decided he needed to strengthen the resolve of lawmakers who were wary of supporting a tax increase in an election year. He told the state legislature to "blame me" for the tax increase. The legislature went on to pass the plan.

As head of the National Governors' Association (1985–86), Alexander again focused on education. The group issued a report that called on governors to focus on improving education by increasing teacher responsibility and accountability and by giving parents more opportunity for school choice.

Alexander won approval three times to raise the state's gasoline taxes to help pay for road construction and improvement projects, which were used to lure new businesses to the state. Despite these increases, Tennessee's overall tax burden remained on the low side when compared to other states.

But some observers say Alexander's efforts to reform education and spur job growth came at the expense of other pressing issues, such as tending to the state's ailing prison system and addressing tax reform.

"He doesn't take on a fight unless he thinks he can win it," commented Erwin Hargrove, a political scientist at Vanderbilt University

. . . Governor of Tennessee

in Nashville. "He's not a politician with a lot of courage."

Alexander has been criticized for his handling of the state's prison crisis, particularly after a federal takeover of the system in 1985 because of overcrowding and inadequate sanitation and health care, which had sparked prison riots.

As governor, Alexander pushed education reform, but critics say he short-shifted prisons.

In response to the 1985 federal ruling, which barred the state's wardens from accepting any more inmates until prison populations were cut, Alexander and the legislature met in a special session. They developed a plan that included lighter and alternative sentences, early release provisions and a prison-construction program.

"Class X" Sentencing

Some critics say part of the overcrowding problem was caused by the Alexander administration's "Class X" sentencing program, which imposed mandatory prison terms for violent criminals. They say the governor and the legislature put the bill into place without adequately taking into account its effect on prison space. Alexander, however, said Tennessee's prisons system was already under a federal order when he came into office and that the remedies he attempted, such as double-celling prisoners, were rejected by a federal court.

"Fixing the prisons was not my No. 1 priority," he said. "It didn't get most of my attention, but it was in better shape when I left than when I came in."

In 1993, he launched the Republican Exchange Satellite Network, which featured a monthly television show to discuss GOP ideas and philosophies. The program enabled him to introduce himself to party donors across the country.

Observers say he has a knack for coming up with catchy phrases to help sell himself or his ideas. In one of his earliest brushes with politics, he used signs that read, "Let's go far ... with Lamar!" in a successful campaign for governor of the Tennessee American Legion Boys State while in high school.

Alexander's political career began in earnest in the mid-1960s when he worked on Howard H. Baker Jr.'s successful first campaign for the Senate. It was the beginning of a long and fruitful relationship.

In 1969, Alexander went to work in President Richard M. Nixon's administration as an executive assistant to Bryce Harlow in the White House's congressional liaison's office.

He left in 1970 to help run the victorious gubernatorial campaign of Tennessee Republican Winfield Dunn, and four years later he sought the office himself. He won the primary but lost in the general election, in part because of the anti-Republican backlash stemming from the Watergate scandal.

Alexander decided to try again in 1978, and this time he shelved his suits and ties in favor of a more folksy image. He began wearing his now famous red and black lumberjack shirt (the one he wore to announce his candidacy in February 1995) and embarked on a 1,000-mile walk across Tennessee, staying in the homes of people across the state, a style he would revive in the 1990s on his drive across the country.

He prevailed over three other Republicans to claim the nomination and went on to victory in the general election over Democrat Jake Butcher, a millionaire banker. Alexander easily won re-election four years later.

Alexander was only the second Republican governor to win the governorship in Tennessee since 1920 (with Dunn being the other). But his coming to office made national news for another reason.

Federal authorities informed him that the departing governor, Democrat Ray Blanton, was engaged in a cash-for-clemency scheme in the waning days of his term. The state constitution allowed the

Baker: A Major Influence

Although he served in the Cabinet of President George Bush, presidential candidate Lamar Alexander probably owes more politically and professionally to his longtime mentor and friend, Howard H. Baker Jr. (Senate 1967–85, minority leader 1977–81, majority leader 1981–85).

Howard Baker

"I couldn't have picked a teacher with better instincts," Alexander has written. "Watching Howard Baker taught me that politics requires all the gall a person can muster."

Alexander also has acknowledged Baker was a "heavy influence" on his proposed six-month time limit on sessions of Congress. Baker pushed that concept in the 1970s and 1980s.

Alexander worked on Baker's first successful Senate bid in 1966, staying on as a legislative assistant for two years before leaving to join the Nixon administration. When Baker became the Republican leader in 1977, Alexander rejoined his staff as a special counsel. Alexander was elected governor of Tennessee in 1978 and worked hard in behalf of Baker's unsuccessful presidential campaign in 1980.

When he left the Education Department in 1993, Alexander joined Baker's law firm, where his duties allow him to spend most of his time on the trail while providing him with a substantial salary. Baker is also part of Alexander's Finance Group, the campaign's inner circle of fundraisers.

Baker and Alexander both hail from small towns in East Tennessee where a traditional, mainstream Republicanism has marked local politics since the 1800s. Both men were known for working successfully with Democrats and building bipartisan coalitions.

Some of Baker's staff from the 1980 race now form the core of Alexander's organization. Among them are senior adviser Rob Mosbacher, son of former commerce secretary Robert A. Mosbacher, and Ted Welch, a former national GOP finance chairman and now the lead figure in Alexander's fundraising.

newly elected governor to take office, so Alexander took the oath three days prior to the scheduled inauguration. Blanton objected, but other Democratic officials supported the early transfer of power.

Despite having to deal with a Democratic-controlled legislature during both of his two terms, Alexander achieved his goal "to take an embarrassed state and help it succeed and grow," as he described it.

Friends and colleagues say Alexander relished his role as the state's chief executive.

"It's what he's best at," said Tom Ingram, Alexander's chief of staff for more than half of his tenure as governor. "He decides what are a very few goals and really focuses on them."

Alexander described his own style in similar terms. "My way of leadership is to limit the agenda, develop a strategy and be as persuasive as I can."

Alexander, for the most part, had good relations with the Democratic legislature.

"Basically, it wasn't that unpleasant," recalled Tennessee Democratic Party Chairman Will Cheek. "He wasn't horribly partisan. The consensus was that if he could've, he would've won a third term."

Tennessee law limits governors to two terms.

State Rep. John Bragg, a Democrat, said Alexander "was not a negative. He was a plus," but added that he "depended a great deal on public relations."

After luring Nissan's $779 million auto plant for Smyrna in 1980, Alexander used that achievement to persuade GM a few years later to build its $5 billion Saturn plant in Spring Hill, saying the state offered automakers the most competitive playing field anywhere.

In addition to attracting Nissan, Alexander was aggressive in persuading other Japanese companies to do business in Tennessee.

In his 1986 book, *Friends: Japanese and Tennesseans*, Alexander noted that "by early 1985 10 percent, or $1.2 billion, of all Japanese investment in the 50 United States was in one state: Tennessee."

After leaving the governor's mansion and spending six months in Australia with his family, Alexander took a new approach to his concentration on education, taking over as president of the University of Tennessee.

Alexander's Races

Election	Total Expenditures	Percent of Vote
1982		
Alexander (R)	$3,995,942	59.6
Randy Tyree (D)	2,627,734	40.4
1978		
Alexander (R)	2,073,436	55.6
Jake Butcher (D)	4,688,206	44.0
1974		
Ray Blanton (D)	N/A	55.4
Alexander (R)	N/A	43.8

While heading the university system, Alexander focused on fundraising and developing a long-range plan to raise the university's profile and attract better students and faculty members. But while he took the long view from the start, some observers say he had just become comfortable in his position when he left to become Bush's top man on education issues.

"He was just getting to understand the job, getting to where he thought he could be effective," said Jim Haslam, a member of the University of Tennessee board of trustees.

Alexander replaced Education Secretary Lauro F. Cavazos in 1991. The nomination was seen as a positive step toward restoring credibility to Bush's claim that he was the "education president." It was a goal articulated in Bush's 1988 acceptance speech at the GOP national convention, and it was not destined to be the phrase by which Bush would be remembered.

Nonetheless, Alexander said he hopes that phrase will be applied to his presidential record someday.

Even before he was confirmed, however, Alexander had to deal with a hornet's nest stirred by an Education Department official.

The Candidate . . .

At first, my walk embarrassed quite a few establishment Republicans: playing my old high-school trombone—or sometimes a washboard—in "Alexander's Washboard Band," a rag-tag collection of four University of Tennessee band members and me! Wearing the same red-and-black flannel shirt each and every day even to dinners, even in the summer, even on TV!

The 1,000-mile walk, day after day after day, became my metronome, a practiced discipline that infused me with the music of the lives of the people I sought to serve. For the first time ever, I possessed that incandescence that voters see in a candidate with a sense of purpose.

The flannel look Alexander wore when announcing for president was first featured in a walk across his home state.

—*On Alexander's 1978 walk across Tennessee for his successful bid for governor, from his 1988 book,* Six Months Off: An American Family's Australian Adventure *(pp. 48–49)*

Some people in public life may arrive better prepared, but no one rises to the occasion as well as Howard Baker. And he has always had a gift for being partisan and ambitious without seeming to be either.

—*On former Senate Republican leader Howard H. Baker Jr. of Tennessee, from his 1986 book,* Steps Along the Way: A Governor's Scrapbook *(p. 32)*

I was ready to resign in 1984 if the Better Schools Program did not pass. My idea was that Lt. Gov. John Wilder would serve as governor, and I would run in a special election in November 1984 and put the issues straight to the people: Shouldn't we pay teachers more for teach-

... In His Own Words

ing well? Is it tolerable for one-third of the eighth-graders in Tennessee not to know eighth-grade skills? Will you pay higher taxes for excellence? Was I right to veto teacher pay raises just for more of the same?

—On his battle to pass his Better Schools Program, an education reform plan. From Steps Along the Way *(p. 136)*

The negotiations were complex, frustrating, and interminable, but in October 1980 I finally got a call from Marvin Runyon, the ex-Ford executive who was hired to run the Nissan plant. "Lamar," he said. "We're coming to Tennessee." My smile was a foot wide. It was the biggest news in our state in a long time.

—Alexander on luring Nissan Motor Co. to build its new auto plant in Tennessee, from his 1986 book, Friends: Japanese and Tennesseans *(p. 150)*

Someone asked me yesterday if the new Republican Congress is going too far. Just the reverse. I am afraid it will be too timid. The greatest danger Republicans have is this: now that we have captured Washington, we must not let Washington capture us.

—From Alexander's speech in his hometown of Maryville, Tenn., announcing his candidacy for the 1996 GOP presidential nomination

I admire Newt's leadership. He has a general sense of where the country should go. But I would go further.

—From a March 27, 1995, speech in Atlanta

I'm not a Washington conservative. . . I was an activist conservative governor. I was busy getting things done. . . . Because I was an activist, because I was pro-civil rights and because maybe I have a more temperate demeanor than some other people, sometimes people are surprised by my conservative positions.

—From an interview with Congressional Quarterly *on April 25, 1995*

Responding to questions about the candidacy of California Republican Gov. Pete Wilson, who dropped out Sept. 29, 1995:

For the life of me, I can't figure out how he can explain away his contract with the people of California. . . . I was faced with that in 1983 when President [Ronald] Reagan asked me to run for the Senate. I thought about it for a day and I said I can't do that.

—From an interview with Congressional Quarterly *on April 25, 1995*

The official's policy initially sought to ban race-based scholarships at post-secondary schools receiving federal aid. At his confirmation hearing, Alexander said that policy statement had "sent off exactly the wrong signal."

After a seven-month review of such scholarships, however, Alexander announced a policy that would allow colleges to consider race in awarding scholarships but would bar scholarships based solely on race.

Much of his focus while at the department was on Bush's highly publicized "America 2000" plan. It called for voluntary national standards and tests in five core subjects; funding for states to develop school-choice policies; permission for schools to ignore federal rules to raise achievement levels without risking the loss of federal funds; grants to merit schools; encouragement for schools to provide merit pay for teachers; and the raising of private funds to build non-traditional schools.

But Alexander was unable to duplicate the success he had in Tennessee when he tried to sell a plan to the Democratic-controlled Congress.

"Congress was intransigent and uncompromising and out to humiliate Bush," said Diane Ravitch, assistant secretary of education research and improvement under Alexander.

During the Clinton administration, the plan evolved into "Goals 2000" and was passed by Congress in 1994. Alexander, however, said the Clinton administration "turned a national movement into a federal program."

Keith Geiger, president of the National Education Association, disagrees with Alexander's assessment of Goals 2000.

He also said that while his organization took exception to some of Alexander's approaches to improving education, he "was one of the innovators in educational reform."

The Outsider

In his campaign for the White House, Alexander has said he would like to abolish the Education Department, an idea that confounds Geiger and others.

Alexander outlined his plan for abolishing the department in joint testimony he gave with former Reagan administration education secretary William J. Bennett before a House subcommittee Jan. 26, 1995. Under the plan, most of the money for elementary and secondary education—a $12.7 billion authorization for fiscal 1995—would be sent back to the states as a block grant. Other federal departments would handle duties such as student loans and anti-discrimination efforts. What would remain would be a federal education adviser in the White House who would help states by pointing out problems or opportunities in education.

This is part of Alexander's agenda to put more power and decisions into the hands of state and local officials and attack what he calls the "arrogance of Washington."

In all, he said he would start by sending about $200 billion worth of federal programs, including welfare and Medicaid, to the states, as well as most job training programs and law enforcement duties.

In portraying himself as an outsider, Alexander likes to say that the biggest difference between himself and Dole and Gramm is that after his stints in Washington, "I went home."

He also stressed his experience as a chief executive, saying, "There is an enormous difference between what a good chief executive does and what a good chief legislator does."

Like most of the other announced candidates, Alexander has recognized the power conservatives now have in the Republican Party. In addition to wanting to cut the size of government, he has taken a no-new-tax pledge and has said he believes that he can balance the budget and cut taxes.

He has been accused of shunning his moderate image and embracing a conservative message. Alexander disputed that assessment.

"I would describe myself as an activist conservative governor in the 1980s, a governor in the 1980s a lot like [GOP Govs.] Tommy Thompson [of Wisconsin] and John Engler [of Michigan] have been in the 1990s," he said. "I was advocating school prayer, school choice and a balanced budget."

David A. Keene, head of the American Conservative Union, said that even though Alexander describes himself as a conservative he does not offer conservatives much reason to support him.

"The real problem that Alexander has . . . is that at the end of the day there isn't a good reason to be for him," Keene said.

Tennessee's Favorite Sons

In the 19th century, Tennessee was in a class with Virginia and Ohio as a home state for presidents, claiming Andrew Jackson, James K. Polk and Andrew Johnson as favorite sons. In the past generation, the Volunteer State has at least been a fertile source of candidates.

During the 1950s, two Democratic senators from Tennessee were competing for space on the national stage, Estes Kefauver and Albert Gore Sr., father of Vice President Al Gore.

Kefauver became famous holding high-profile hearings on crime and corruption as chairman of the Senate Special Crime Committee. He had strong grass-roots support, especially in the West and Midwest, but his moderate views on civil rights marked him as a maverick in the South.

Kefauver won the 1952 New Hampshire primary in an upset that hastened President Harry S. Truman's retirement. He won most of the remaining primaries and led on the first two ballots at the convention. Then party leaders organized a draft of former Illinois governor Adlai E. Stevenson, which succeeded on the third ballot.

Kefauver ran again in 1956, slogging through the primaries with Stevenson all the way to California before conceding defeat. At the convention, Stevenson left the selection of his running mate to the delegates, setting off a scramble between Kefauver and his in-state rival, Gore. The duel was complicated by the emergence of Massachusetts John F. Kennedy, who came within a handful of votes of winning before Gore settled the matter by withdrawing in favor of Kefauver. The Stevenson-Kefauver ticket was soundly defeated that fall by Republicans Dwight D. Eisenhower and Richard M. Nixon.

The younger Gore entered the Democratic primaries in the 1988 cycle when he was not yet 40 years old. He skipped the Iowa caucuses and made only a half-hearted effort in New Hampshire, focusing his campaign on the South and West. He split the Super Tuesday primaries almost evenly with Massachusetts Gov. Michael S. Dukakis and Jesse Jackson. However, Gore could not translate his appeal to other sections of the country. He pulled out after a third-place showing in New York.

Gore returned to New York on a happier note in 1992, when he was tapped by Bill Clinton to be his running mate.

Alexander's stance on abortion also may dissuade conservatives from supporting him.

While claiming to be an abortion opponent and supporting the right of states to restrict abortion, he has said the federal government should have no role in the abortion issue and, therefore, should "not subsidize it, encourage it or prohibit it."

"Certainly, he won't get support from the pro-life community," said Carol Long, the political action committee director for the anti-abortion National Right to Life Committee.

Grasping the Nettle

Former Sen. Baker has been a strong influence in Alexander's life and is one of the strongest backers of his bid for the White House. He has called Alexander a "protege of sorts" and has said that he has "extraordinarily high regard for him."

Alexander's "cut their pay and send them home" idea—which he pushed heavily before the election of a Republican Congress in 1994—was inspired by Baker, who said for years that Congress should meet for only six months. Alexander added the kicker of proposing that Congress also have its pay cut in half.

But Baker's support for his efforts to secure the Republican nomination for president—a position Baker sought for himself in 1980 and once planned to seek again in 1988—is more tangible.

Alexander was hired in 1993 by Baker's law firm, Baker, Donelson, Bearman & Caldwell, to advise a few handpicked clients at a salary of $295,000 a year.

"I recruited him to the firm," Baker said, acknowledging that the firm set up a careful arrangement with Alexander to "leave him free to pursue his political ambitions."

Alexander's arrangements with Baker's firm and other financial ventures, however, have raised eyebrows, even though they appear to be legal. In 1995, the newly merged Lockheed Martin paid Alexander $236,000 as part of a buyout deal because his services as a Martin Marietta Corp. director were no longer needed.

Since his nomination hearings to be education secretary, Alexander has been plagued by questions about financial deals that have made him a millionaire. Senators were concerned about revelations that Alexander had earned large sums of money with little investment as governor and at the University of Tennessee.

Erwin Hargrove, a political scientist at Vanderbilt University, said Alexander's financial deals raise questions not of legality but of appearance, suggesting Alexander has had "blinders" on.

Alexander said he does not believe such deals have left an unseemly impression with the public, even in the wake of intense scrutiny of investments made by the Clintons.

"I think my business career and my investments ... will be an asset rather than a liability," he said.

Ready Money

Gramm has boasted of having the "most reliable friend" one can have in politics, "ready money." But Alexander is also on good terms with that friend.

While he cannot boast wide name recognition, Alexander has built a strong organization and fundraising team.

Helping to lead his fundraising efforts is Ted Welch, a former Republican National Committee finance chairman who is widely viewed as highly skilled.

Alexander's first-quarter financial statement filed with the Federal Election Commission showed that his campaign had total receipts of $5.26 million—a figure that then stood second only to Gramm's.

Polls may continue to show Alexander lagging far behind, but GOP leaders say he has built strong grass-roots organizations in the key states of Iowa and New Hampshire.

"He's got some excellent people in the field," said Marlys Popma, the political director for the Iowa Republican Party (who has since left to work with Gramm).

With Dole expected to win the Iowa caucuses next February, "the race in Iowa is for second or third," and it is wide open for those two spots, she said.

In New Hampshire, Alexander is credited with having one of the best organizations of any of the GOP candidates.

Alexander took to the airwaves early by holding a town meeting broadcast by the state's major television station.

Despite critics who dismiss his chances of emerging from the pack to claim the nomination, Alexander seems assured that if he has "the opportunity to present my message to the tens of millions of people who will be voting in the primaries . . . I'm convinced if I do that I will be nominated."

Patrick J. Buchanan

Patrick J. Buchanan ran a short-lived but sharp-edged campaign for president in 1992 that left incumbent President George Bush wounded and bleeding. Having thus proved that he can bite as well as bark, the former speechwriter and commentator enters the 1996 race with his sights trained on another Republican front-runner he considers insufficiently conservative.

With Senate Majority Leader Bob Dole of Kansas so far ahead of the early pack, Buchanan himself admits his candidacy is a "long, long shot." Unlike other candidates such as Sen. Phil Gramm of Texas and former Tennessee governor Lamar Alexander, Buchanan does not seem bent on winning the nomination so much as on other political goals. He has said his aim is to create a "winning Republican coalition" by combining social and religious conservatives with economic populists who feel threatened by immigrants and international trade.

It is far from clear that Buchanan can unite these groups, or that such an alliance, once forged, could secure him a place on the 1996 ticket. But surviving even the first round of delegate-selecting events in 1996 would assure him of a voice in national affairs well beyond that of an ordinary columnist and TV commentator.

Buchanan also matters to the 1996 campaign because he can be counted on to keep the water boiling in certain pots other Republicans would just as soon let simmer. Potentially divisive issues such as abortion, school prayer, immigration and affirmative action are conspicuous by their absence in the House GOP's Contract with America, the document that has driven political debate throughout 1995.

Patrick J. Buchanan

Republican of McLean, Va.
Born: Nov. 2, 1938; Washington, D.C.
Education: Georgetown University, A.B., 1961;
M.S., Columbia University, 1962.
Family: Wife, Shelley Ann.
Religion: Roman Catholic.
Political career: Sought 1992 GOP nomina-
tion for president.
Professional career: Editorial writer, *St. Louis
Globe-Democrat,* 1962–66; aide and speech-

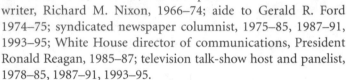

writer, Richard M. Nixon, 1966–74; aide to Gerald R. Ford
1974–75; syndicated newspaper columnist, 1975–85, 1987–91,
1993–95; White House director of communications, President
Ronald Reagan, 1985–87; television talk-show host and panelist,
1978–85, 1987–91, 1993–95.

If Republicans do not bring these issues more to the fore, some
social conservatives say they will look to launching an alternative
party in the presidential election of 1996.

A more likely scenario, however, is that these voters and the organizations that speak for them will remain within the Republican
tent but demand satisfaction. Religious conservatives are widely
estimated to account for up to 40 percent of the GOP primary electorate, which makes them essential to any GOP nominee in November and a rich prize for any candidate in the primaries. At one time,
their social-conservative candidate of choice was thought to be former Vice President Dan Quayle. When Quayle declined to run,
some thought the beneficiary would be Gramm. But to date,
Gramm has not been able to lock up much of this support.

"The market is still open for religious voters," said Mike Russell, a
spokesman for the 1.6 million-member Christian Coalition, a byprod-
uct of the 1988 presidential campaign of televangelist Pat Robertson.

Buchanan is not likely to corner this market, but he is both an
avid bidder and a potential winner in it.

"Pat is at a critical point," said Gary L. Bauer, a policy adviser in the Reagan White House and now president of the Family Research Council, a conservative think tank and lobbying group. "A lot of people are toying with joining his campaign," he noted. "Pat could really jell."

Tantalizing Signs

Buchanan is already running second to Dole in some national polls, including one widely publicized survey done in late April by the *New York Post*. Even though Republicans have nominated their early front-runner in every election since World War II, Buchanan believes Dole "will be seen as a figure of the past" and ultimately dismissed in favor of the candidate who runs second to Dole in the early going.

Political observers in key battleground states rate Buchanan's chances high. "Right now, I'd say the presumption is Bob Dole will carry Iowa, but second place is a prize well worth having and second place is wide open," said Iowa Republican Chairman Brian Kennedy, who gives credit to Buchanan for already having a good organization in the state.

Buchanan's best 1992 showing came in New Hampshire, traditionally the state that holds the first primary. Sen. Judd Gregg, R-N.H., speculated May 8 that Buchanan could finish a strong second to Dole there if he wins the endorsement of the *Manchester Union-Leader*, the state's largest and most politically influential newspaper (and a Buchanan ally in 1992).

The *Union-Leader* ran an editorial in April praising Buchanan for bringing spice to the race and "forcing others to contend with a wider range of issues."

The paper has been harshly critical of Gramm, perceiving in him a less-than-total commitment to the state primary's "first in the nation" status. Later, the paper endorsed Buchanan outright.

But Gramm has other problems on the right, as well. Although still considered the leading challenger to Dole, he has been widely criticized by social conservatives for seeming reluctant to campaign on non-fiscal issues.

"Gramm easily could have had all the social conservatives," said Robert X. Johnson, parliamentarian of the Texas GOP. "But Gramm threw away half his base of support," Johnson said, by refusing to rule out a pro-abortion rights running mate and giving little weight to abortion as a campaign issue.

"I have a 100 percent pro-life record," Gramm boasted at an Arizona appearance, but he is nevertheless chided by anti-abortion activists for hiding that light under a bushel. "The average American isn't going to look at your voting record, they need to hear you verbalize it," Beverly LaHaye, president of the Concerned Women for America, recalled counseling Gramm. "If you don't, nobody's going to know how you voted."

Gramm was unable to allay these concerns fully in two highly publicized appearances at the conservative Heritage Foundation in Washington and at evangelist Jerry Falwell's Liberty University in Virginia. On both occasions, he restated his opposition to abortion rights and to homosexuals serving in the military, along with his support for school prayer. Gramm "made a good cut at the plate," said Russell, but "we'll see how he continues to press these themes."

Gramm got a letter of commendation after these speeches from James Dobson, president of Focus on the Family, who had been one of his more persistent critics. But Dobson, too, withholds judgment, saying "We're not going to be satisfied with being thrown a bone occasionally."

That is why Buchanan has a chance to score with the committed social conservatives by emphasizing their agenda more strongly than any other candidate with national name recognition.

"Trying to move out in front of the pack, you've got to hit the rhetorical scale with notes that command attention," said Charles Dunn, a Clemson University political scientist.

Hitting notes that command attention has been Buchanan's forte since he was writing speeches for presidential candidate Richard M. Nixon in the 1960s. But this particular ability to appeal to activists may also limit Buchanan's appeal to the larger electorate.

In recent years, for example, he has referred to Capitol Hill as "Israeli-occupied territory" and called Adolf Hitler "an individual of great courage." Accused of anti-Semitism during the 1992 campaign, Buchanan denied any such beliefs. But the issue was raised again when Buchanan announced his candidacy and hecklers from

1992 GOP Primary Results

Patrick J. Buchanan never came close to winning a primary in 1992, but he helped vivify dissatisfaction with President George Bush within Republican ranks.

Date	State	Bush	Buchanan
Feb. 18	New Hampshire	53.0%	37.4%
Feb. 25	South Dakota	69.3	30.7
March 3	Colorado	67.5	30.0
	Georgia	64.3	35.7
	Maryland	70.1	29.9
March 7	South Carolina	66.9	25.7
March 10	Florida	68.1	31.9
	Louisiana	62.0	27.0
	Massachusetts	65.6	27.7
	Mississippi	72.3	16.7
	Oklahoma	69.6	26.6
	Rhode Island	63.0	31.8
	Tennessee	72.5	22.2
	Texas	69.8	23.9
March 17	Illinois	76.4	22.5
	Michigan	67.2	25.0
March 24	Connecticut	66.7	21.9
April 7	Kansas	62.0	14.8
	Minnesota	63.9	24.2
	Wisconsin	75.6	16.3
April 28	Pennsylvania	76.8	23.2
May 5	District of Columbia	81.5	18.5
	Indiana	80.1	19.9
	North Carolina	70.7	19.5
May 12	Nebraska	81.4	13.5
	West Virginia	80.5	14.6
May 19	Oregon	67.1	19.0
	Washington	67.0	19.6
May 26	Arkansas	87.4	12.6
	Idaho	63.5	13.1
	Kentucky	74.5	25.5
June 2	Alabama	74.3	7.6
	California	73.6	26.4
	Montana	71.6	11.8
	New Jersey	77.5	15.0
	New Mexico	63.8	9.1
	Ohio	83.3	16.7
June 9	North Dakota	83.4	—
TOTAL		72.5%	22.8%
Delegate votes at convention		2166	18

a Jewish political organization leapt onto the dais to denounce him as a racist.

"There's a firm line between the political cutting edge and what is objectionable, and all too often Pat crossed it," writes Quayle in his book *Standing Firm*. But what offends an establishment politician such as Quayle may sound like music to the ears of some disaffected voters.

Buchanan can attract voters—and repel others—not solely through the purity of his commitment, but through the intensity of his fervor as well.

When Buchanan, who has never held elective office, announces repeatedly from the stump, "I will be the most pro-life president in the history of the United States of America," no one seems to doubt him. "I have a contract with the unborn," Buchanan said in a May 11 interview.

Other candidates have raised the issue of illegal immigration, particularly temporary entrant Pete Wilson, the governor of California, but Buchanan is leading the Republican charge against what he calls "an invasion of the country." As in 1992, Buchanan is proposing building a "Buchanan fence" along 200 miles of the U.S.Mexico border, which he claims will cut illegal immigration by 95 percent.

Buchanan is alone in the field in calling for a five-year moratorium on all immigration, throwing into the mix the halt of legal immigrants. Buchanan has "put all the other candidates on notice," said Daniel Stein, executive director of the Federation for American Immigration Reform. "We believe Buchanan has expressed a yearning in the American electorate for immigration reform."

Buchanan calls for a federal law based on the California's Proposition 187, which bars illegal immigrants from receiving most government benefits, saying: "It's outrageous that American taxpayers, as hard-pressed as they are . . . have to provide social welfare benefits for those whose accomplishments are to break the laws to get into the United States and to get on welfare."

"This issue could elect Pat," said Peter Brimelow, author of *Alien Nation*, a 1995 book about the country's immigration problems. "People have no idea how powerful this idea is once it gets into the political system."

According to Buchanan, "a 20 percent decline in real working income" over the last 20 years is a "direct consequence" of immigrants who "widen the labor pool," coupled with "unfair trade treaties and idiotic trade policies."

Buchanan stands nearly alone among the GOP candidates in opposition to the North American Free Trade Agreement, the General Agreement on Tariffs and Trade and the bailout of the Mexican peso (which he called "a rip-off of the taxpayers").

"If we conducted our arms negotiations as we're conducting our trade negotiations," he said, "we'd all be speaking Russian now."

Well before the Clinton administration slapped tariffs on a few Japanese luxury cars in reaction to Japanese trade practices, Buchanan was pushing for aggressive measures.

In a May 10 op-ed piece in the *New York Times*, Buchanan advocated a 10 percent tariff on all Japanese goods entering the United States. He said the next day that this move would "return more jobs to America," helping "those who work with their hands and tools."

The resulting expansion of the tax base "in the valleys up in New Hampshire ... in the Rust Belt," and elsewhere, Buchanan said, would provide enough revenue for him to eliminate corporate income taxes on all businesses with assets under $25 million.

"Pat Buchanan is the one guy in the Republican field who understands trade and how important it is," said Rep. Duncan Hunter, R-Calif.

Campaign lore has it that Buchanan found his economic populist heart campaigning in New Hampshire shortly after announcing his first bid on Dec. 10, 1991.

Visiting a paper mill in Groveton, N.H., where 350 people had been laid off earlier in the day, Buchanan approached a line of workers awaiting their Christmas turkeys. Buchanan was awkward initially, but one man looked at him and said, "Save our jobs."

Declaring his candidacy this year, Buchanan recalled that incident and said it had convinced him that government "is frozen in the ice of indifference" when it comes to workers' problems. Although Buchanan was clearly moved by the recession's human toll in New Hampshire, as early as 1970 he wrote Nixon an 11-page memo advising him to exploit politically the populist resentments of the working class.

Citizen Buchanan Mostly Known . . .

Since the Warren Court outlawed prayer in the public schools, surveys have shown Americans supporting a constitutional amendment, if necessary, to restore it. . . . And the parables of Christ remain prohibited in the same high schools where the racist drivel of Eldridge Cleaver is deemed to be "relevant."

For generations now there has beaten within the liberal heart the utopian dream that by placing inner-city black children in schools with white children, the former will pick up the habits and ambitions of the latter—even as they might the Hong Kong flu. Racial amity will be advanced, and racial peace assured. It does not work.

—*From his 1975 book,* Conservative Votes, Liberal Victories

When we say we will put America first, we mean also that our Judeo-Christian values are going to be preserved and our Western heritage is going to be handed down to future generations and not dumped into some landfill called multiculturalism.

—*From his declaration of candidacy, Dec. 10, 1991*

There are only two groups beating the drums for war in the Middle East: the Israeli defense ministry and its amen corner in the United States Senate.

—*From* The McLaughlin Group, *Aug. 24, 1990*

I think God made all people good, but if we were to take a million immigrants in, say Zulus, next year, or Englishmen, and put them in Virginia, what group would be easier to assimilate and would cause less problems for the people of Virginia?

—*From ABC's* This Week with David Brinkley, *Feb. 9, 1992*

Mr. Bush, you recall, promised to create 30 million jobs. He didn't tell us he would be creating them in Guangdong Province, Yokohama or Mexico.

—*From a 1992 stump speech*

Now if you belong to the Exeter-Yale GOP club, that's not going to bother you greatly because, as we know, it is not their children who get bused out of South Boston into Roxbury; it is not their brothers who lose contracts because of minority set-asides; it is not the scions of Yale and Harvard who apply to become FBI agents and construction work-

... For What He Says—and How

ers and civil servants and cops, who bear the onus of this reverse dis-crimination. It is the sons of middle America who pay the price.... If I am elected, my friends, I will go through this administration, depart-ment by department and agency by agency, and root out the whole rot-ten infrastructure of reverse discrimination, root and branch.

—On the 1991 Civil Rights Act, at the annual Conservative Political Action Conference, Feb. 21, 1992

There is a religious war going on in this country for the soul of America. It is a cultural war as critical to the kind of nation we shall be as the Cold War itself, for this war is for the soul of America. And in the struggle for the soul of America, [Bill] Clinton and [Hillary] Clinton are on the other side and George Bush is on our side.

—From his Republican National Convention speech, Aug. 17, 1992

I will use the bully pulpit of the presidency of the United States to the full extent of my powers and ability to defend American traditions and the values of faith, family and country from any and all directions. And together, we will chase the purveyors of sex and violence back beneath the rocks whence they came.

—From his declaration of candidacy, March 20, 1995

I think we cannot tolerate millions of illegal immigrants coming into America every year, driving down wages, taking our jobs, using social welfare benefits, bankrupting states.

—At a campaign appearance, March 31, 1995

The surgeon general of the United States is America's family doc-tor. You cannot have an abortionist as America's family doctor.

—Reacting to the confirmation hearings of Dr. Henry W. Foster Jr. as surgeon general on Fox Morning News, *May 8, 1995*

Ronald Reagan was pro-life and won two landslides. George Bush won in '88, landslide; he was pro-life. The one way to kill the Republi-can Party and to split it again, as we did in 1992, is to walk away from life and have the right-to-life folks walk out and go into a third party of social conservatives. If the Republican Party walks away from life, the Republican Party will split.

—From McLaughlin's One on One, May 14, 1995

"We should aim our strategy primarily at disaffected Democrats, at blue-collar workers, and at working-class ethnics. We should set out to capture the vote of the 47-year-old Dayton [Ohio] housewife," Nixon recalled in his 1978 memoir.

Buchanan would later offer similar advice to President Ronald Reagan, stressing the political emotions of the disaffected. Through years of print and broadcast editorializing, Buchanan has been a bulwark of conservative populism. He was an early advocate of term limits, not only for members of Congress but for federal judges as well.

But if all the right holes have been punched in Buchanan's "outsider" credentials card, he has spent virtually his entire adult life in the swim of Washington's media and political life.

Buchanan, one of nine children, grew up in Blessed Sacrament Parish on the northwest side of Washington near the Maryland line. "Our hometown was the sleepy and segregated city of Washington, D.C.," Buchanan wrote in his 1988 autobiography, *Right from the Beginning.* It was "a quiet pleasant place that has since disappeared." Buchanan, who now lives in a suburb across the Potomac River in Virginia, has since decried "these guys playing bongo drums . . . [in] the town I grew up in."

After a four-year stint writing editorials at the *St. Louis Globe-Democrat,* Buchanan was hired by Nixon as an aide in 1966. Buchanan stayed with Nixon until the end of his presidency.

Buchanan began a profitable career in 1975 as a pundit, writing a syndicated newspaper column. By 1978, he was appearing on television panel shows and traveling the country as a speaker. He returned to the White House to serve as Reagan's communications director from 1985 to 1987. After that, his TV work included two stints as co-host of CNN's *Crossfire* and as a regular panelist on *The McLaughlin Group.* When he gave up all this to run for president in 1992, journalist Robert Scheer reported Buchanan was walking away from an annual income of $800,000.

Buchanan's effort peaked early. Exit polls from the 1992 New Hampshire primary erroneously suggested that he had taken 42 percent of the vote to Bush's 48 percent. That was virtually identical to the 1968 showing Sen. Eugene J. McCarthy made in New Hampshire against President Lyndon B. Johnson, forcing the president from the race. News reports trumpeted Buchanan's vote as a great moral victory over Bush, even though the actual Buchanan share later turned out to be just 37 percent.

Buchanan knew he could not force Bush from the race with moral victories alone, so he targeted Georgia as a state where he might actually win. But Bush won Georgia easily, and Buchanan's share of the vote there actually declined from New Hampshire.

Other primary states where he had not campaigned as vigorously gave Buchanan nearly as much support as Georgia, suggesting that he was attracting votes largely as a vehicle for expressing dissatisfaction with Bush.

Undaunted, Buchanan took his case to Michigan, another economically depressed state where he thought his "America First" message might resonate. But Michigan voters were turned off by his wife's Mercedes-Benz and his own references to Cadillacs as "lemons."

The Bush campaign, slow to respond to the Buchanan challenge at first, ran a television ad showing Buchanan driving the offending vehicle. Angela "Bay" Buchanan, the candidate's sister and close adviser, recommended he call a news conference and take a sledgehammer to the car, but Buchanan rejected the advice.

His vote share dropped to 25 percent in Michigan, but Buchanan stayed in the race until the convention, still talking about Bush's breaking a "no new taxes" pledge.

At the Republican National Convention in August, in a prime-time address that served as his introduction to millions of Americans, Buchanan attacked Bill Clinton's patriotism and said Clinton was on the wrong side of "a cultural war . . . for the soul of America."

Quayle and others felt Buchanan had hurt Bush's re-election effort with his combative convention speech.

Clemson's Dunn suggests that Buchanan will always "hit his head on a low ceiling of support" because his message is not positive. And, as it turned out, Clinton's campaign as "the man from Hope" proved more in tune with the populace's mood in 1992 than Buchanan's vision of cavalry troopers "taking back" the country "block by block."

But the mood of the electorate in the next cycle may well be closer to the conservative anger that carried Republicans to congressional majorities in 1994. No declared candidate in 1996 has associated himself more closely with that mood than Buchanan.

Bob Dole

Whether or not Senate Majority Leader Bob Dole is elected president in 1996, his achievements in the first eleven months of 1995 are a pinnacle few could have imagined for him even a few short years ago.

Late in 1992, with the White House about to fall to the Democrats and the Senate elections just as gloomy for the GOP, the Kansas Republican spoke bitterly of ending his long career. Dole saw nothing but frustration ahead if the number of minority Senate Republicans was going to be "down in the 30s somewhere."

But Dole persevered. In the 103rd Congress he led a highly successful rear guard action against President Clinton and the majority Democrats. His immediate reward was a historic midterm election in 1994 that produced the most Republican Congress in nearly half a century.

After eight years as Senate minority leader, Dole has returned to the majority with his parliamentary skills undiminished.

He proved that in June 1995, when he scuttled Clinton's most prominent nomination of the year (Dr. Henry W. Foster Jr. for surgeon general), eclipsed the efforts of a presidential rival (Sen. Phil Gramm, R-Texas) to do the same, struck a bargain with House Speaker Newt Gingrich, R-Ga., guaranteeing a budget resolution with a tax cut and a balanced budget (by 2002) and saw through the Senate a monumental revision of telecommunications law—all in the span of seven days.

Dole, 72, has emerged as the clear front-runner for the Republican presidential nomination in 1996—a year when that nomination may well be the inside track to the White House.

Bob Dole

Republican of Russell, Kan.
Born: July 22, 1923; Russell, Kan.
Education: University of Kansas, 1941–43;
Washburn University, A.B. 1952, LL.B. 1952.
Family: Wife, Mary Elizabeth Hanford; one
child.
Religion: Methodist
Political Career: Kansas House, 1951–53; Rus-
sell County attorney, 1953–61; U.S. House,
1961–69; Republican nominee for vice pres-
ident, 1976; sought Republican nomination for president, 1980,
1988; U.S. Senate, 1969–present.
Occupation: Lawyer
Military Service: Army, 1943–48.

In three national polls done for news organizations in June, Dole led Gramm, his closest rival, by at least 30 percentage points. In Iowa, site of the first delegate-selecting caucuses, Dole's lead was 40 points.

Some predicted that Dole's numbers would waste away before Christmas or be shattered by Dole's first failure to meet expectations. Some erosion in the polls was visible in Dole's favorability rating, which typically fell below 50 percent, but the nominating dynamic of any cycle can be unpredictable.

"Dole is where the smart money might be now," says Fred Greenstein, a political science professor at Princeton University and a leading scholar of presidential politics. "It's hard to see anything or anyone that stands dramatically in his way. But the current primary process continues to be full of surprises."

Greenstein says conversations with his colleagues leave him particularly cautious about the "sharply compressed" calendar for choosing delegates to the nominating convention in 1996. Because several of the largest states have moved their voting dates into March—including California and New York—more than two-thirds of the delegates will be chosen by the end of that month.

"You have to take a lead like this at least somewhat at face value," argues Burdett Loomis, professor of political science at the University of Kansas and a longtime Dole watcher.

"The surprise is that no one of the fiftyish generation has really emerged yet," adds Loomis. "But if there's a vacuum, Dole can fill it with a lot more than just seniority. He has substance, and he has a lot of IOUs, and he has to be taken seriously."

Early leads have been known to evaporate for Democratic presidential hopefuls, but Republicans have tended to honor order and seniority to the degree that winning the nomination has been a matter of knowing one's time and waiting one's turn. In every cycle since 1940 the Republicans have nominated the presidential contender who entered the election year as the best known and most widely supported in opinion polls. Barring a health problem or an unforeseen reversal of equal gravity, Dole will be the one to beat.

"More and more, the nomination is being determined by what happens in the year before the primaries," says political scientist Paul Green of Governors State University in Illinois. "What's more, I don't see anyone else besides Dole with the bench strength to survive if he takes a hit early."

Dole knows survival. He came back from mortal wounds in World War II and a three-year ordeal in Veterans Administration hospitals. He entered politics in 1950 while still an undergraduate on the GI bill and has held elected public office continuously since.

This will be his fourth time around in presidential politics, having been the vice presidential nominee in 1976 and an entrant in the primaries in 1980 and 1988. The difference is that this time he is the front-runner. That fact has enabled him to raise more money at the start of his campaign (more than $13 million in the first six months of 1995) than in the 1988 cycle (when he had raised less than $4 million at the comparable juncture).

But rather than protect his lead, Dole has elected to press his advantage. He might have stepped down as majority leader of the Senate and campaigned full time as his party's senior statesman. Instead he has chosen to brave the slings and arrows in an era of great controversy and intraparty struggle.

After Years of Building Consensus . . .

Through 35 years in Congress, Bob Dole has been known as a negotiator and a legislative broker, a master of the inside compromise that gets the job done. Small wonder that his own philosophy has been described as an "ideological blur."

As the leader of congressional opposition to President Clinton, Dole toughened his stand on issues almost across the board. Now, with the 1996 presidential nomination on the line, he has striven to prove his fealty to conservative doctrine—not only on taxes, government spending and foreign policy, but also on gun control, civil rights and abortion.

Gun Control

Dole has gone back and forth on gun control. As a House member, he voted for the Gun Control Act of 1968; as a senator in the mid-1980s, he supported efforts to weaken that act's restrictions.

During Republican President George Bush's term, Dole supported a crime bill that prohibited the production, sale and possession of semi-automatic assault weapons. As recently as 1991, he supported a version of the Brady Bill, which imposed a waiting period for the purchase of handguns and a mandatory background check on purchasers.

After the Clinton's election, Dole no longer felt obliged to seek a middle ground. He voted against a second consideration of the Brady Bill and against banning 19 semiautomatic weapons.

Dole has hardened his line against gun control in the 104th Congress, competing directly for the votes of National Rifle Association members and other Second Amendment enthusiasts. A recent *Los Angeles Times* poll estimated that gun owners would constitute 48 percent of the Republican primary vote. Although many of these votes may already belong to Dole's rival for the presidency, Sen. Phil Gramm of Texas, the competition is not over.

Civil Rights

On civil rights, Dole moved to the left in the mid-1960s but soon returned to a conservative line. In the 1980s, he adopted a middle-of-the-road position and worked to pass the civil rights bill of 1991.

Dole voted for both the 1964 Civil Rights Act and the 1965 Voting Rights Act. The next year, however, Dole conspicuously reversed his

... Dole Takes Uncompromising Stance

position and voted against the Civil Rights Act of 1966 and the Equal Employment Opportunity Act of 1966.

Dole seemed to shift again when he came to the Senate. Although he consistently voted against forced busing to desegregate schools, he supported the 1975 extension of the Voting Rights Act, and he became something of a champion for civil rights bills in the 1980s.

In 1983, Dole led the floor fight to make Martin Luther King Day a national holiday. He voted in favor of the Civil Rights Act of 1991, a bill that sought to reverse a series of Supreme Court decisions that had made it difficult for workers to win job discrimination suits.

Affirmative Action

In 1995, Dole made headlines by pressing an attack on affirmative action programs authorized under a presidential order issued in 1965.

In 1985, Dole had been one of 69 senators who asked President Ronald Reagan not to rescind that same order. Among others urging retention of the order at that time was Dole's wife, Elizabeth, who was then Reagan's secretary of transportation.

Abortion Issues

Dole consistently votes against abortion rights supporters, but he has softened his rhetoric since the 1970s. In 1983, he voted to overturn the Supreme Court decision that legalized abortion, and in 1986 he supported an amendment to tax-overhaul legislation that would have taxed nonprofit clinics and hospitals that perform abortions. The measure did not pass.

In 1990, he voted against a measure that allowed minors to seek abortions without parental notification; in 1992, he voted to lift the fetal tissue research ban but against abortion counseling at federally funded clinics. In 1994, he voted against the act that safeguarded access to abortion clinics.

His rhetoric, however, has become significantly less aggressive. In 1989, Dole called for a more moderate party stance on the abortion issue; he said he feared that rejecting members who advocate abortion rights could divide the Republicans. Dole also agreed with the position that abortion is permissible in cases of rape, incest or when the woman's life is in danger.

At the same time, Dole has shown himself willing to do what he must and to sacrifice what he must to assure himself of the nomination. He has returned to his own conservative roots on social issues such as gun control, civil rights and welfare. He has strenuously courted moral activists by taking on sex and violence in Hollywood—and by extension the humanism and permissive attitudes that are anathema to religious conservatives. And he has voluntarily signed a pledge not to raise taxes, shrugging off the curse some believe cost him the nomination in 1988.

Meeting the Minuses

The knock on Dole as a national campaigner has been threefold. Conservative purists call him a pragmatist who lacks an overarching ideology. His campaigns have lacked organization, both nationally and at the local level. And he has had a burdensome reputation for being acerbic to the point of meanness. This last trait has been exacerbated by his frequent inability or unwillingness to curb his own tongue.

Dole will never be the champion of those conservatives who have been described over the years as the New Right, "movement conservatives" or, most recently, "Contract Republicans," so named for the House GOP's Contract with America.

Dole will never be entirely forgiven for the tax bills he pushed on President Ronald Reagan as chairman of the Senate Finance Committee in 1982 and 1983, nor the things he said about tax-cutting "supply-side" economics and its enthusiasts along the way. (Example: "A busload of supply-siders went off a cliff; the bad news is there were two empty seats.")

Specific issues aside, it seems implausible that a Republican electorate enamored of term limits and fresh faces in Washington would turn over the White House to a man who has been in government without interruption for 45 years and in Congress for 35 of them—a man who is the second longest-serving Republican on Capitol Hill.

But Dole by most measures has been a consistent conservative. His annual rating from the liberal Americans for Democratic Action has usually been below 10 (and never higher than 22). He rose to national politics as an acolyte of President Richard M. Nixon, and

House and Senate Candidacies

Election	Votes	Percentage
1992 General (Senate)		
Bob Dole (R)	706,246	63
Gloria O'Dell (D)	349,525	31
Others	70,676	6
1992 Primary (Senate)		
Bob Dole (R)	244,480	80
R. W. Rodewald (R)	59,589	20
1986 General (Senate)		
Bob Dole (R)	576,902	70
Guy MacDonald (D)	246,664	30
1986 Primary (Senate)		
Bob Dole (R)	228,301	84
S. J. Ashley Landis (R)	42,237	16
1980 General (Senate)		
Bob Dole (R)	598,686	64
John Simpson (D)	340,271	36
1980 Primary (Senate)		
Bob Dole (R)	201,484	82
1974 General (Senate)		
Bob Dole (R)	403,983	51
William R. Roy (D)	390,451	49
1968 General (Senate)		
Bob Dole (R)	490,911	60
W. I. Robinson (D)	315,911	39
1966 General (House)		
Bob Dole (R)	97,487	69
Berniece Henkel (D)	44,569	31
1964 General (House)		
Bob Dole (R)	113,212	51
Bill Bork (D)	108,086	49
1962 General (House)		
Bob Dole (R)	102,499	56
J. Floyd Breeding (D)	81,092	44
1960 General (House)		
Bob Dole (R)	62,335	59
William A. Davis (D)	42,869	41
1960 Primary (House)		
Bob Dole (R)	16,033	45
Keith Sebelius (R)	15,051	42
Philip J. Doyle (R)	4,423	12

How Dole Voted . . .

Congressional Quarterly each year selects a series of key votes on major issues and records how every member voted on each. The following examples were culled from Dole's 35-year career on Capitol Hill.

1995	Allow vote on Henry Foster as surgeon general	N
	Approve balanced-budget constitutional amendment	N
	(switched vote to N to permit motion to reconsider)	
	Approve budget resolution eliminating deficit by 2002	Y
1994	Safeguard access to abortion clinics	N
	End U.S. arms embargo on Bosnia	Y
	Approve national education standards	N
	Approve balanced-budget constitutional amendment	Y
	End U.S. trade embargo on Vietnam	N
1993	Require unpaid family and medical leave	N
	Provide incentives to limit campaign spending	N
	Pass Clinton budget with new taxes and cuts	N
	Allow the president to decide on gays in the military	N
	Reduce spending for the anti-missile program	N
	Provide foreign aid with aid to Russia	Y
	Allow federal abortion funding	N
	Limit subpoena of Packwood diaries	Y
	Ban certain semiautomatic assault weapons	N
	Approve national "motor voter" registration bill	N
	Approve five-day waiting period for handguns	N
	Approve NAFTA	Y
	Approve budget increasing taxes and reducing deficit	N
1992	Provide extended unemployment benefits	Y
	Oppose deeper cuts in spending for SDI	Y
	Reject stricter nuclear power licensing procedures	Y
	Impose 9-month moratorium on nuclear testing	N
	Override family and medical leave veto	N
	Reduce enterprise zones and IRA deductions	Y
	Allow abortion counseling at federally funded clinics	N
	Provide $26.5 billion for foreign assistance	Y
	Override veto of cable TV rate cap bill	N
	Reauthorize water projects in Utah and California	Y
	Approve school-choice pilot program	Y
1991	Approve waiting period for handgun purchases	Y
	Raise senators' pay and ban honoraria	Y

...On the Major Issues

	Tie China's trade status to human rights progress	N
	Pass Civil Rights Act of 1991	Y
1990	Oppose prohibition of some semiautomatic weapons	N
	Adopt constitutional amendment on flag desecration	Y
	Oppose requiring parental notice for minors' abortion	N
	Halt production of B-2 stealth bomber at 13 planes	N
1989	Oppose barring federal funds for "obscene" art	N
	Allow vote on capital gains tax cut	Y
1988	Approve death penalty for drug-related murders	Y
	Oppose workfare amendment to welfare overhaul bill	N
1987	Limit testing of anti-ballistic missiles in space	N
	Confirm Supreme Court nominee Robert H. Bork	Y
1986	Block chemical weapons production	N
	Impose sanctions on South Africa	N
	Aid Nicaraguan contras	Y
1985	Weaken gun control laws	Y
	Produce MX missiles	Y
1984	Permit school prayer	Y
	Cut military aid to El Salvador	N
1983	Overturn Supreme Court decision legalizing abortion	Y
	Create Martin Luther King Jr. holiday	Y
1982	Increase gasoline tax 5 cents per gallon	Y
	Cut $1.2 billion for public works jobs	Y
	Retain tobacco price supports	Y
	Impose sanctions on South Africa	N
1981	Disapprove sale of AWACS planes to Saudi Arabia	N
	Index income tax rates against inflation	Y
1980	Block Justice Department busing suits	Y
	Approve military draft registration	N
1979	Guarantee loans for Chrysler Corp.	Y
	Impose moratorium on nuclear power plant building	N
1978	Approve treaty giving Panama Canal to Panama	N
	Raise mandatory federal retirement age from 65 to 70	Y
1977	End federal price controls for onshore natural gas	Y
	Kill plan to cap outside income at 15% of Senate pay	Y
1974	Impose death penalty for certain crimes	Y
	Kill amendment to ban busing for desegregation	N
1972	Equal Rights Amendment	Y
	Antiballistic Missile Treaty with the Soviet Union	Y

he was chosen as President Gerald R. Ford's running mate in 1976 largely to cover Ford's right and appeal to Sun Belt Republicans.

And while he has adopted a variety of positions on affirmative action, civil rights, guns and some other social issues, he has been a consistent opponent of abortion and a consistent supporter of school prayer. Most important at the present, he has shown great willingness to work with the Christian Coalition and other religious groups eager to effect changes in federal statutes.

Tellingly, conservative Christian activists also have reached out to him. When the Christian Coalition brought forth its 10-point agenda at the Capitol in May, other Republican leaders came to the news conference; Dole waited in his office for Ralph Reed and other Coalition leaders to come to him. He was cordial and welcoming but did not commit himself to all of the coalition's Contract with the American Family.

Still, Dole is clearly loath to offend these forces in the party. He and his wife, Elizabeth, have stopped attending the Foundry United Methodist Church in Washington (where the Clinton family goes many Sundays). The Associated Press reported in May that the Doles were seeking an evangelical church because the minister at Foundry, a supporter of feminism and gay rights, was too liberal. The Doles refused comment. Elizabeth Dole, president of the American Red Cross, had become a member at Foundry during the tenure of an earlier minister.

All on the Altar

As for his campaign organization, Dole is finally benefiting from the dynamic that makes all front-runners look well-organized and well-financed. He has also been successful at turning bad stories around with a minimum of damage. When adviser Edward J. Rollins made a joking reference to two Jewish members of Congress as "Hymie boys," he was separated from the campaign.

When questions were raised about contributions to a think tank ancillary to Dole's political organization, Dole quickly closed the fund. The Better America Foundation returned about $2.5 million that was left from more than $4.6 million collected from corporations and wealthy individuals since its founding in 1993.

The mean-streak criticism is muted, at least for the moment, by Dole's own somewhat cooler demeanor. This restraint contrasts with the hot talk coming from other Republicans in the new Congress, including Gingrich and Gramm, as well as from talk-show hosts and commentators in general.

But if Dole seems to have his personal demons under control, he gains only so long as he keeps them under control. The floor leader was clearly straining to keep his cool early in July when confronted with a filibuster mounted awkwardly by Sens. Paul Wellstone, D-Minn., and Carol Moseley-Braun, D-Ill.

"This debate doesn't make any sense to me," Dole growled as he glowered at Wellstone.

But the front-runner must know that the day his temper flares in a debate or at a media event, he will see all his worst moments replayed on television again and again.

He hurt his own cause in 1976 by referring to the four wars Americans had fought in the 20th century as "Democrat wars." He warned his Senate colleagues in 1985 to pass the Gramm-Rudman deficit reduction law fast or else "people may start to read it." And in 1988 he seemed to scotch his own fading chance for the nomination when he snapped at New Hampshire primary winner George Bush: "Stop lying about my record."

But in the 1996 cycle, in a last hurrah he himself might have thought impossible after 1988, the well-seasoned Dole strives to apply all the lessons he has learned. He seems finally willing to put it all on the altar, holding back nothing—not even his right to speak his mind in blunt terms.

Time to Remember

There is another side to the new, more controlled Dole, something beyond mere self-restraint. It is a newfound willingness to talk about his own past, his youth and most especially his wartime wounds. The shift was made plain when Dole made his official declaration in April on the 50th anniversary of the week when his life nearly ended on a battlefield in northern Italy.

In the waning days of World War II, as a second lieutenant in the Army, Dole was part of an assault on well-entrenched German

CQ Vote Studies . . .

Participation: The percentage of recorded votes for which Dole was present and voting.

Presidential Support: The percentage of votes on which Dole agreed with the public position of the president.

Party Unity: The percentage of votes on which Dole agreed with the majority of Republicans voting against a majority of the opposing party.

Conservative Coalition: The percentage of votes on which Dole stood with a majority of Republicans and Southern Democrats against a majority of Northern Democrats.

Year	Voting Participation	Presidential Support		Party Unity		Conservative Coalition	
		S	O	S	O	S	O
Senate							
1994	99	35	65	95	4	97	3
1993	98	28	72	95	5	88	7
1992	99	88	12	94	6	92	8
1991	100	96	4	93	7	98	3
1990	100	80	20	86	14	95	5
1989	99	94	4	89	11	87	13
1988	86	68	19	70	12	86	5
1987	95	71	24	85	10	81	6
1986	99	92	8	92	7	95	4
1985	99	92	7	92	6	92	5
1984	97	90	9	90	8	96	2
1983	96	78	21	88	8	89	7

troops that left every man in his platoon wounded. Dole was caught in machine gun fire and an explosion that shattered his right shoulder and arm and broke five vertebrae. After hours on the ground, he was dragged to safety by another soldier. When Dole reached a hospital back in the United States, he had lost more than 60 pounds, one kidney, all use of his right arm and most of the feeling in his left. He endured more than three years of surgery and rehabilitation in

... Bob Dole

Year	Voting Participation	Presidential Support		Party Unity		Conservative Coalition	
		S	O	S	O	S	O
1982	98	86	13	91	8	85	10
1981	98	85	7	94	5	92	5
1980	96	48	49	72	24	77	20
1979	93	39	57	78	16	85	14
1978	95	32	65	77	19	83	14
1977	97	53	44	85	12	89	8
1976	78	66	17	71	12	77	6
1975	93	75	16	86	8	90	5
1974	89	63	33	71	21	76	17
1973	96	71	27	83	14	89	10
1972	92	87	4	87	3	88	1
1971	86	80	13	89	9	87	4
1970	94	81	15	88	8	86	7
1969	94	75	21	80	12	87	7
House							
1968	85	42	46	84	7	88	0
1967	94	40	53	90	10	91	4
1966	99	37	63	90	10	100	0
1965	99	34	63	91	7	98	2
1964	99	27	73	94	6	100	0
1963	99	23	76	100	0	93	7
1962	98	33	65	93	5	94	0
1961	99	15	83	88	12	100	0

Note: S—supported; O—opposed.

a succession of VA hospitals. Half a century later, he still has no use of his right arm and less than full feeling in his left.

He carries a pen or a paper in his right hand to deflect handshakes, reaching out to grip proffered hands with his left. "I do try harder," Dole once said. "If I didn't, I'd be sitting in a rest home, in a rocker, drawing disability [benefits]."

Dole did not return to the University of Kansas, where before going to war he had been a track star with thoughts of medical school. Instead he went to Washburn University in Topeka, where he could finish his bachelor's degree and work toward a law degree at the same time. He got both degrees magna cum laude in 1952, by which time he had also sought and won his first public office—a seat in the Kansas legislature.

He left that seat after one term to be county prosecutor back in his hometown of Russell, where his father had run a cafe, then a grain elevator and later a small creamery. Dole's mother had taken in sewing and sold Singer sewing machines door to door. The Doles had been Democrats, and their son admitted admiring President Franklin D. Roosevelt. But western Kansas was Republican ground, and Dole entered public life in the GOP.

After three re-elections as prosecutor, he made his first bid for Congress in 1960. The Republican nomination was tantamount to election, and Dole won it by 982 votes.

Dole's four terms in the House were marked by a focus on the Agriculture Committee, where hard work and cooperation enabled a young member of the minority to have some effect. He voted with his party on nine out of 10 votes and usually took part in the conservative coalition of Republicans and Southern Democrats—except that he voted for both the Civil Rights Act of 1964 and the Voting Rights Act of 1965. He opposed the creation of Medicare in 1965, as did most Republicans, as well as the Equal Employment Opportunity Act of 1966.

In 1968, Dole sought the seat of a retiring GOP senator and easily defeated a former governor in the primary. It was a GOP year most everywhere, and Dole won that November with 60 percent of the vote.

Arriving in the Senate in 1969, the first year of Nixon's presidency, Dole soon found a role as a floor debater willing to defend his party's new president. His eagerness for such combat put off his party elders in the Senate, especially Minority Leader Hugh Scott of Pennsylvania, but it stood him in good stead with other Republicans.

Nixon tapped Dole to be chairman of the Republican National Committee in January 1971, and the same bulldog tendencies would lead to a spot on the 1976 national ticket.

Interest Group Ratings

These ratings represent the percentage of votes Bob Dole cast in agreement with each group's stated position on test votes selected by the groups. The groups are the liberal Americans for Democratic Action, the conservative Americans for Constitutional Action (1961–80), the American Conservative Union (1981–94), the AFL-CIO and the U.S. Chamber of Commerce (1965–94).

Year	ADA	ACA/ACU	AFL-CIO	USCC
Senate				
1994	0	100	0	90
1993	10	88	0	100
1992	5	93	17	90
1991	5	86	17	80
1990	0	83	33	75
1989	5	86	0	88
1988	15	91	33	91
1987	5	77	20	83
1986	0	91	0	89
1985	0	91	10	90
1984	10	86	0	83
1983	5	64	19	56
1982	15	80	20	62
1981	5	76	11	100
1980	22	77	28	90
1979	21	64	21	75
1978	20	58	22	83
1977	5	70	11	88
1976	10	87	16	75
1975	17	67	24	75
1974	19	84	18	80
1973	10	82	27	78
1972	0	84	10	100
1971	4	71	17	100
1970	13	76	17	80
1969	0	64	18	80
House				
1968	0	90	25	100
1967	7	96	9	100
1966	0	93	0	100
1965	0	89	0	100
1964	8	95	9	—
1963	0	100	9	—
1962	0	91	0	—
1961	0	92	0	—

President Gerald R. Ford was trailing Democratic challenger Jimmy Carter in the summer of 1976, and Dole seemed a good choice as his point man in the attack plan for that fall. Dole also had ties to the Western populist wing of the party, which was disappointed that the nomination had not gone to Ronald Reagan that year.

Dole ripped into Carter, while Ford stayed in the Rose Garden. The gap in the polls narrowed steadily, but not without cost. Dole's performance in his debate with Democrat Walter F. Mondale created a firestorm of criticism, not only for "Democrat wars" but for shots Dole took at Carter's *Playboy* interview and for Dole's weak defense of Ford's pardon of Nixon. When the Ford-Dole ticket lost, Dole got much of the blame for losing and little credit for making it close.

The bad press did not deter him from another national campaign just four years later. Although his own seat was up and the list of Republican aspirants was long, Dole entered the early presidential contests in 1980. But he had trouble getting out of Washington to campaign and wound up with an astonishingly negligible 597 votes in the New Hampshire primary (out of nearly 150,000 cast). He pulled out, endorsed Reagan and filed for re-election.

But once again, Dole's descent into a valley simply lead to a new peak. The GOP seized not only the White House but the Senate in 1980, and Dole, re-elected with 64 percent of the vote, became chairman of the Finance Committee. In that job he would win wide favor for passing Reagan's tax cuts in 1981 and a hail of disapproval for the tax increases he crafted in subsequent years to reduce the ballooning budget deficit. Gingrich, then a second-term back bencher in the House, labeled Dole "a tax collector for the welfare state"—a dart that stuck.

Nevertheless, Dole stepped up immediately when the majority leader job came open late in 1984. Four others ran, including three who are still in the Senate—Ted Stevens of Alaska, Pete V. Domenici of New Mexico and Richard G. Lugar of Indiana (now a rival bidder for the GOP presidential nomination). Dole survived to the final ballot with Stevens and narrowly prevailed, in part with the support of conservative gadfly Sen. Jesse Helms, R-N.C.—whose heavy use of floor privileges Dole pledged to preserve.

Dole's first tour as the Senate's ringmaster (1985–86) had its highs and lows. "You have to produce and you have to provide leadership," Dole would say, and he paid the price to do both.

Beyond the legislation that passed with his help—including a major tax code revision, a new immigration law, a five-year farm bill and aid to the Nicaraguan contras—he overcame the small groups of senators who had been bringing the chamber's business to a standstill. His success rested on the palpable sense of his will to use what power he had. During the floor consideration of South Africa sanctions in 1985, Dole had the official copy of the legislation locked in a safe, temporarily preventing further action. Bitterly denounced on another occasion by Democratic leader Robert C. Byrd of West Virginia, Dole shot back: "I did not become majority leader to lose."

The loss of the Senate majority in 1986 freed Dole to concentrate on what he privately called "the other thing," the party's 1988 nomination for president. He spent more time on the road, but remained as the Republican leader in the Senate throughout the campaign cycle. Some believed this showed Dole's lack of confidence in his own chances, but for Dole, the issue was demonstrating his willingness and ability to lead.

Dole has made the same call in the current cycle. If the president can run for re-election while serving as president, he asks, why should the Senate leader not seek promotion while continuing to do his job? For Dole, wielding power—with all its risks and challenges—is the best audition there could be for all the power, risks and challenges of the presidency.

For those who view politics less as an ideological test and more as a confrontation between personalities, Dole will always be formidable. Those who measure first the man will be struck by how he has endured, rising repeatedly from the graves others have dug for him. The years have elevated him beyond regionalism, above his days as someone else's hit-man and beyond the usual definitions of liberal and conservative.

One Last Lesson

All this could have been said of Bob Dole the last time he made a run for the presidential nomination. What is different now is that

Bob Dole and . . .

President Richard M. Nixon had enormous influence over the politics of the postwar era in American history, and one of the ways he wielded that influence was by elevating the career of Bob Dole.

The two first met in the 1950s. In the mid-1960s, when Nixon was traveling the country repairing the damage from his losing campaigns of 1960 and 1962 (when he ran for president and governor of California, respectively), he came to Kansas twice to help Dole win re-election to the House. The journalist Richard Ben Cramer, in his study of the 1988 presidential candidates, quotes Dole as remembering Nixon as "the only guy in Washington who remembered to shake with his left hand." (Dole lost the use of his right hand to his World War II wounds.)

Nixon

The alliance persists even now. In May 1995, the *Los Angeles Times* reported that Dole "has leaned heavily on detailed advice from Nixon, one of his oldest and closest political friends" prior to the former president's death in 1994.

Among other things, Nixon urged Dole to run "as far as you can to the right because that's where 40 percent of the people who decide the

Elizabeth Dole

nomination are." After that, Nixon was said to have advised, "you have to run as fast as you can back to the middle, because only about 4 percent of the nation's voters are on the extreme right wing."

Bonding in 1969

Dole was first elected to the Senate in 1968, the year Nixon first won the White House. As a freshman in the exclusive chamber, Dole found his first role as the new president's most ardent and frequent defender.

Dole was among the few who fought hard for Nixon's ill-fated Supreme Court nominees, F. Clement Haynsworth Jr. in 1969 and G. Harrold Carswell in 1970. One Nixon aide described the 47-year-old Dole as "a hungry Doberman pinscher."

... The Nixon Connection

When Dole was named the new Republican National Committee chairman in January 1971, he embarked on a nonstop traveling schedule that would bring him his first real national attention and bring his 24-year marriage to an end in 1972. (Dole's first wife, Phyllis, told reporters that after he took the RNC job Dole was home for dinner just twice in an entire year.)

Ford

Dole was at odds with Nixon's campaign staff in 1972, constantly urging that the president ought to do more to help other Republicans. His reward was to be eased out of the RNC chairmanship early in 1973. That turned out to be fortunate because the Nixon presidency would soon be destroyed by the Watergate scandal.

Dole continued to defend Nixon until the president resigned. But having established his distance from the Nixon White House, he also could joke that "Watergate happened on my night off" and get away with it.

Bob Dole (1973)

Lasting Benefits

Dole emerged from that era with two benefits of incalculable importance. He established his bona fides as a loyal and indefatigable combatant with President Gerald R. Ford, Nixon's successor, who would choose Dole as his running mate in 1976.

Moreover, in the Nixon administration, Dole met a woman from North Carolina (a former Democrat) who had sub-Cabinet rank and an obvious future of her own in politics. Elizabeth Hanford would become secretary of transportation for President Ronald Reagan and secretary of labor for President George Bush, but in 1975 she became the second wife of Bob Dole.

Advising Dole nearly 20 years later, Nixon would say the Kansan had the "brains, heart and guts" to be president.

Loyal to Nixon to the end, Dole gave a tearful eulogy at Nixon's funeral in which he said the second half of the 20th century would be known as "the Age of Nixon."

Senate Majority Leader Bob Dole and House Speaker Newt Gingrich, left, worked hard to foster intra-party unity following the November 1994 elections, which produced the most Republican Congress in nearly half a century.

he has internalized one more great lesson: that he cannot win the nomination with just the votes of those who appreciate his finer skills as a legislator.

The very qualities that professionals appreciate most—such as Dole's ability to reach in all directions in crafting and negotiating a deal—arouse suspicion among the partisans who decide who gets the party nomination. Obviously mindful of this problem, Dole in the past few years has shown more fealty to party principle.

The game of the nomination is played with what Princeton's Greenstein calls "a deck full of wild cards." But for now, at least, Dole has more right than anyone to look to November 1996 and a presumed match-up with Clinton.

This raises yet a final difference between Dole's current circumstances and those of the 1988 campaign. In that era, Dole was running to succeed a personally popular president whose special qualities of charm and unifying, upbeat energy he could not hope to reproduce.

In this cycle, Dole has the great advantage of contrasting himself against a president of relative youth (24 years his junior) whose personal history from draft avoidance to vacillations in the Oval Office may well make Dole's age and gravitas more attractive than ever before.

Phil Gramm

Phil Gramm was beaming. Surveying the Texas-size crowd filling the Dallas Convention Center for his lavish February fundraiser, he had good reason. On the eve of announcing his candidacy for the White House, Gramm supporters were dining on beef filet and jumbo shrimp as far as his eyes could see. Introductory speakers had presented a feast of praise for the man Texas GOP Gov. George W. Bush declared had "entered the big leagues." Best of all, the record-breaking take for the evening was more than $4 million, cementing Gramm's position as the best-financed entrant in the 1996 field.

Gramm has often framed his campaign as a classic fight for the little guy, but on this night in Dallas he paid homage to his wealthier supporters. "I have the most reliable friend you can have in American politics," he observed, "and that is ready money."

Virtually all serious presidential aspirants combine money-raising prowess with an appeal to the average American. For Gramm, who talks like a Texas populist even as he breaks bread with a network of corporate donors, the two roles seem to share the stage at once.

Gramm's career from boyhood to the Senate has been a story of such contradiction and confounded expectations. He failed three grades, but turned himself around in military school and went on to earn a doctorate in economics. He entered academia as a less than blue-chip prospect but rose to a tenured teaching position. He came to politics as a hopeless long shot who survived a party switch to become the biggest vote-getter in what is now the nation's second most populous state. Despite his well-crafted outsider image, Gramm served for two election cycles as chairman of the National

Phil Gramm

Republican of College Station, Texas
Born: July 8, 1942; Fort Benning, Ga.
Education: University of Georgia, B.B.A. 1964, Ph.D. 1967.
Family: Wife, Wendy Lee; two children: Marshall and Jefferson.
Religion: Episcopal.
Political career: Sought Democratic nomination for U.S. Senate, 1976; U.S. House, 1979–85; U.S. Senate, 1985-present.
Professional career: Economics professor, Texas A&M University, 1967–78; partner, Gramm & Associates, 1971–78.

Republican Senatorial Committee—forging relationships with party insiders from coast to coast.

At home, he built a reputation for taking credit for government projects while cultivating a national reputation as a cold-steel budget slasher. He has promised to balance the federal books in a single White House term, but he has not released a plan for doing it—or endorsed anyone else's. Gramm has shown a remarkable ability to knit the seemingly disparate pieces of his persona into a coherent and compelling whole. The unanswered question of the Gramm presidential bid is whether the fabric of this political identity will hold.

Most Likely to . . .

During his nearly two decades inside the Beltway, first as a Democrat-turned-Republican in the House and now as the senior senator from Texas, Gramm has cultivated a national reputation as the man most likely to buck the Washington establishment.

On the heels of the 1994 elections, Gramm is positioning himself as the GOP presidential hopeful most in tune with the party's new majorities in Congress. He wants to be seen as the most likely candidate to carry the spirit of 1994 into the campaign of 1996.

Gramm has long styled himself as a candidate of change, a man who would provide a new direction in American politics and a radical overhaul of the federal bureaucracy. Now that a restive Republican electorate seems to be swinging his way on the issues, Gramm is determined not to let any rival candidate capture his moment.

In the early months of the campaign, Gramm has shown no tendency to moderate. Instead, he has lived up to his hard-edged reputation for being perpetually on the offensive. He has contrasted himself with his chief rival for the nomination, Senate Majority Leader Bob Dole of Kansas, whom he casts as a compromising insider.

"After the 1994 election, I have become convinced that the American people are ready for a real conservative," Gramm said April 9 on CNN. "People want somebody who is not a deal-cutter, who is not a straddler, somebody who is willing to stand up and fight."

As Gramm confidently draws the line between his campaign and Dole's as a choice between revolution and moderation, the Texan's presidential bid grows naturally from his roots as a missionary for the activist wing of the Republican Party. Like House Speaker Newt Gingrich of Georgia, Gramm has tied his political fortunes to the rise of the conservative movement in American politics. Like the media-focused Speaker, he has risen on his masterful ability to market his ideas in the context of the modern Congress.

While all the presidential candidates in the GOP field are seeking to capitalize on the 1994 election in some fashion, Gramm's strategy offers the most direct test of the question: Is the vote surge that Republicans rode in 1994 a guide to the winning Electoral College coalition in 1996?

"Are the people serious about what they said in 1994?" asked Jeb Hensarling, Gramm's Washington-based campaign manager. "Have the American people hit their threshold of tolerance? Are they ready to redefine the role of government in a free society? Or do they want to tinker around the edges a little bit?"

Mountains to Climb

While voter sentiment could well work to the advantage of the candidate most committed to a shake-up of the federal establishment, the obstacles for the Gramm campaign are substantial. If

How Gramm Voted ...

Congressional Quarterly each year selects a series of key votes on major issues and records how every member voted on each. The following examples were culled from Gramm's 17 years on Capitol Hill.

1995	Approve balanced-budget constitutional amendment	Y
1994	Safeguard access to abortion clinics	N
	Adopt budget resolution preserving spending levels	N
	Require risk assessments on EPA regulations	Y
	Bar military action in Haiti without Congress' approval	N
	End U.S. arms embargo on Bosnia	Y
	Waive Senate budget rules to allow crime bill vote	N
	Move to vote on voluntary campaign spending caps	N
	Move to vote on lobbying disclosure and gift ban bill	N
	End U.S. trade embargo on Vietnam	N
1993	Require unpaid family and medical leave	N
	Provide incentives to limit campaign spending	N
	Pass Clinton budget with new taxes and cuts	N
	Authorize funds for the National Service program	N
	Confirm Ruth Bader Ginsburg to the Supreme Court	Y
	Allow president to decide on gays in the military	N
	Reduce spending for Missile Defense program	N
	Allow federal abortion funding	N
	Cut U.S. military funding in Somalia	N
	Limit subpoena of Packwood diaries	Y
	Ban certain semiautomatic assault weapons	N
	Approve national "motor voter" registration bill	N
	Approve five-day waiting period to buy handguns	N
	Approve NAFTA	Y
	Approve budget increasing taxes and reducing deficit	N
1992	Provide extended unemployment benefits	Y
	Oppose deeper cuts in spending for SDI	Y
	Reject stricter nuclear power licensing procedures	Y
	Impose nine-month moratorium on nuclear testing	N
	Reduce enterprise zones and IRA deductions	Y
	Allow abortion counseling at federally funded clinics	N
	Provide $26.5 billion for foreign assistance	Y
	Approve school-choice pilot program	Y
	Allow fund shift from defense to domestic programs	N
	Reject lifting fetal tissue research ban	Y

...On the Major Issues

1991	Spend $509 million for superconducting super collider	Y
	Raise senators' pay and ban honoraria	N
	Tie China's trade status to human-rights progress	N
	Kill amendment blocking anti-missile defense system	N
	Shift $3.1 billion to domestic programs from defense	N
	Authorize use of force in Persian Gulf	Y
	Grant 20 more weeks of unemployment benefits	N
	Confirm Clarence Thomas to Supreme Court	Y
	Pass Civil Rights Act of 1991	Y
1990	Oppose prohibiting some semiautomatic weapons	Y
	Adopt constitutional amendment on flag desecration	Y
	Oppose requiring parental notice for minors' abortion	N
	Halt production of B-2 stealth bomber at 13 planes	N
1989	Oppose reduction of SDI funding	Y
	Oppose barring federal funds for "obscene" art	N
1988	Oppose "workfare" amendment to welfare overhaul	N
	Pass civil rights restoration bill over Reagan veto	N
1987	Limit testing of anti-ballistic missiles in space	N
	Oppose banning tests of larger nuclear weapons	Y
	Confirm Supreme Court Nominee Robert H. Bork	Y
1986	Block chemical weapons production	N
	Impose sanctions on South Africa	N
	Amend Constitution to require a balanced budget	Y
	Aid Nicaraguan contras	Y
1985	Weaken gun control laws	Y
	Reject school prayer	N
	Produce MX missiles	Y
1984	Pass bill to revise immigration laws	N
	Freeze physicians' fees under Medicare	Y
1983	Raise Social Security retirement age to 67	Y
	Bar covert U.S. aid to Nicaragua	N
	Pass Equal Rights Amendment	N
1982	Subsidize home mortgage rates	N
	Amend Constitution to require balanced budget	Y
1981	Reagan budget proposal	Y
	Disapprove sale of AWACs planes to Saudi Arabia	N
1980	Approve military draft registration	Y
	Strengthen fair housing laws	N
1979	Weaken Carter oil profits tax	Y
	Approve anti-busing amendment	Y

Gramm boasts proven fundraising ability (his latest campaign spending report indicated that he had raised nearly $19 million counting funds transferred from his Senate campaign account), he is nevertheless battling the nagging status of underdog in a front-loaded primary process likely to be over shortly after it begins.

Since World War II, the Republican presidential nomination has nearly always gone to the candidate who led in polls of the party faithful 18 months before the convention. This time around, that would be Dole. Although Dole lacked solid majority support in early polls by GOP voters, he ran well ahead of the rest of the field. Gramm, meanwhile, often struggled to stay in double-digits and ahead of other contenders in his bid to make it a "two-man race."

Gramm has tried to overcome this by selling himself as a fire-breathing conservative, but so far he has not been able to consolidate support on the right. In part this is because other candidates are contesting the same ground. Dole has taken a no-new-taxes pledge (he had refused to do so in 1988) and has suggested abolishing four Cabinet departments, while moving sharply to the right on gun control and other issues. Political newcomer Malcolm S. "Steve" Forbes Jr. has also been touting Reagan-style economics.

Gramm's best chance to flank Dole might be on the social issues that have increased in importance in recent Republican conventions and platforms. "The Reagan coalition was composed of economic and social conservatives," observed Texas Republican Party Chairman Tom Pauken. "Gramm's primary [focus] has been on economic issues. So social conservatives want to see that some of their concerns are addressed if he is elected."

Here, too, Gramm has yet to consolidate his position on the right. Also bidding for the same ground are Patrick J. Buchanan, who challenged President George Bush in 1992, and two lesser-known but ideologically pure entrants: Alan Keyes and Rep. Robert K. Dornan, R-Calif. All three of these candidates feature their anti-abortion stands more prominently than Gramm does.

A major prize for any of the Republican hopefuls would be the endorsement or informal backing of the Christian Coalition, the powerful organization spawned by the 1988 presidential campaign of evangelist Pat Robertson. So far, the group has withheld its affections. In Iowa, for example, some Gramm organizers have com-

House and Senate Candidacies

Election	Votes	Percentage
1990 General (Senate)		
Phil Gramm (R)	2,302,357	60
Hugh Parmer (D)	1,429,986	37
1984 General (Senate)		
Phil Gramm (R)	3,111,348	59
Lloyd Doggett (D)	2,202,557	41
1983 Special (House)		
Phil Gramm (R)	46,371	55
Dan Kubiak (D)	33,201	40
1982 General (House)		
Phil Gramm (D)	91,546	95
Ron Hard (Libertarian)	5,288	5
1980 General (House)		
Phil Gramm (D)	144,816	71
Dave Haskins (R)	59,503	29
1978 General (House)		
Phil Gramm (D)	66,025	65
Wes Mowery (R)	35,393	35
1976 Primary (Senate)		
Lloyd Bentsen (D)	970,983	63
Phil Gramm (D)	427,597	28

plained that conservative activists they had counted on for early support are holding back, awaiting word from Ralph E. Reed Jr., the coalition's executive director.

Importance of Message

Daunting as it may be to establish one's self as the premier conservative in 1996, Gramm has little choice but to pursue that goal. His conservative message has been at the core of his political success, lifting him from virtual gadfly status to two smashing victories in Senate elections.

Campaign Finance

Election	Receipts	Receipts from PACs	Total Expenditures
1990 (Senate)			
Gramm (R)	$11,626,377	$1,426,839 (12%)	$9,799,104
Parmer (D)	1,674,600	263,762 (16%)	1,677,087
1984 (Senate)			
Gramm (R)	9,863,651	1,479,851 (15%)	9,509,724
Doggett (D)	5,958,008	804,929 (14%)	5,880,512
1983 (House, Special)			
Gramm (R)	942,469	164,145 (17%)	750,299
Kubiak (D)	118,733	500 (0%)	126,008
1982 (House)			
Gramm (D)	822,101	254,653 (31%)	784,901
1980 (House)			
Gramm (D)	262,937	108,195 (41%)	71,161
1978 (House)			
Gramm (D)	552,534	124,487 (23%)	480,778
Mowery (R)	116,411	5,409 (5%)	116,386

"His persona is subordinate to the message," said Bruce Buchanan, a professor of government at the University of Texas at Austin. "That packaging allows him to escape the scrutiny."

The presidential season presents the prospect of greater inspection, including the charge that his years in Washington have made him, despite his protests, a creature of the capital.

"I would say that Phil is clearly a Washington insider," said Rob Mosbacher, a Houston businessman (and son of the former secretary of commerce who was the chairman of Bush's 1992 re-election campaign). The younger Mosbacher, who now supports former Tennessee governor Lamar Alexander for the 1996 nomination, says Gramm "believes that many of our problems can be solved in Washington—by him."

Mosbacher, for example, notes that Gramm supports a federal

response to crime, adding, "If you want to lay on new penalties for crime then you should run for governor or sheriff."

Still, what may stand most squarely in Phil Gramm's path to the office he has long coveted is Phil Gramm himself. Not known for his charisma on the stump, Gramm remains a product of the rough-riding culture of Texas politics. Although his toughness is unquestioned, Gramm lacks the charm that helped President Ronald Reagan overcome voter anxiety about his ideological fervor.

"His ability to emotionally appeal to the American voter is one of the open questions of this campaign," said James B. Francis, who has run Gramm's Senate campaigns and will serve as a senior adviser in the presidential effort.

To some degree, Gramm's personality has been maligned by a Washington establishment he has never courted. While most Washington politicians seek the acceptance of their colleagues, Gramm has seemed to relish and capitalize on their dislike for him. "I did not come to Washington to be loved," he likes to say. "And I have not been disappointed."

Just after winning his first House term in 1978, Gramm came to town from College Station, where he had taught economics at Texas A&M University, and demonstrated a soon-to-be-famous penchant for angering his colleagues. In an early encounter, he had boasted to a colleague that he had brought to Congress the greatest mind the House had known since Stephen A. Douglas, a political rival of Abraham Lincoln in the 1850s.

Knowing When and How

Then, as now, Gramm had a talent for political timing. The 1980 Reagan landslide gave Republicans a majority in the Senate and 192 seats in the House. The swing votes on such key issues as the federal budget rested with Gramm and about 50 other conservative "Boll Weevil" Democrats, nearly all from the South.

After just two years in the House, Gramm understood the budget as well as the most seasoned member. In addition, Gramm had a remarkable understanding of where power resided in Washington—and how to use it. He managed to overcome the shortcomings of his personality with ready-made expertise, impeccable timing and a willingness to exploit alliances.

CQ Vote Studies

Participation: The percentage of recorded votes for which Phil Gramm was present and voting.

Presidential Support: The percentage of votes on which Gramm agreed with the public position of the president.

Party Unity: The percentage of votes on which Gramm agreed with a majority of Democrats (1979–82) or Republicans (1983–present) voting against a majority of the opposing party.

Conservative Coalition: The percentage of votes on which Gramm stood with a majority of Republicans and Southern Democrats against a majority of Northern Democrats.

Year	Voting Participation	Presidential Support		Party Unity		Conservative Coalition	
		S	O	S	O	S	O
Senate							
1994	90	32	56	87	5	88	6
1993	93	21	76	94	2	93	0
1992	94	90	10	91	1	89	5
1991	97	93	4	92	5	90	3
1990	96	78	14	88	8	100	0
1989	97	86	12	91	6	82	16
1988	90	78	15	85	4	92	3
1987	97	87	9	92	5	84	13
1986	98	99	1	95	4	97	1
1985	98	87	13	95	5	88	12
House							
1984	58	37	27	58	5	69	8
1983	81	73	16	79	1	93	0
1982	97	84	14	10	87	89	10
1981	95	75	22	20	77	99	0
1980	96	39	59	24	72	92	4
1979	96	37	61	26	69	91	6

Note: S—supported; O—opposed.

If unvarnished assertiveness defined Gramm's early years in Congress, it was balanced by his uncanny understanding of the rules of the game. When he needed to, Gramm could cajole and curry favor one on one. Conservative GOP Rep. David A. Stockman, R-Mich. (House 1977–81), who became Reagan's budget director, found his Texas colleague an "unexpected, easygoing, brilliant and simpatico new ally." In a book unsparing of virtually everyone in Congress, Stockman wrote: "Deep down in his soul, Phil Gramm was a hard-core anti-spender."

In selling the Reagan budget proposals, Gramm teamed up with Delbert L. Latta of Ohio, the ranking Republican of the House Budget Committee. Trading on his then-Democratic credentials, he helped secure the support of 29 conservative Democrats in the House who played a crucial role in discarding the work of the Budget Committee and other House committees. The House voted instead to accept $37.3 billion in budget cuts known as Gramm Latta II.

Gramm could outmaneuver even the most seasoned House members. He persuaded fellow Texan Jim Wright to champion him for a Budget Committee seat, arguing that his association with budget director Stockman would aid the dialogue between House Democrats and the White House.

Almost immediately, however, Gramm rewarded Wright's patronage with partisan betrayal. Gramm would attend the committee's closed-door Democratic Caucus meetings, then report the details of the proceedings to Stockman.

In 1983, Gramm's colleagues retaliated by bouncing him from the Budget Committee. Lesser politicians might have faltered under the weight of such antipathy, but Gramm understood early on the political potency of demonizing Washington. "I had to choose between Tip O'Neill and y'all," Gramm told admiring crowds in his district. "I decided to dance with the ones that brung me."

Gramm seized this opportunity to switch to the Republican Party, resign his seat and recapture it in a special election. In 1984, when Republican senator John G. Tower retired, Gramm easily won the right to succeed him. In 1990, he spent $9.8 million winning re-election, outspending his opponent by more than 5 to 1.

Pattern Set Early

Gramm first ran a quixotic campaign for the Democratic Senate nomination against incumbent senator Lloyd Bentsen in 1976. Bentsen was distracted by his own brief presidential effort in that cycle, but he still held Gramm to 29 percent of the vote.

In 1978, Gramm ran for the 6th District House seat of retiring Democrat Olin E. "Tiger" Teague. He raised more than $550,000 to overcome the man Teague had preferred in a primary runoff and to win the fall election with 65 percent of the vote.

In the House, Gramm's early career was based on his ability to disrupt the regular order of legislative proceedings and substitute his own agenda for that of more established lawmakers. He understood that if an idea could be packaged in terms the American public could understand, the usual committee process could be finessed. If the feelings of other members were bruised along the way, so be it.

One Texas Republican House member said in 1986 that anyone meeting Gramm quickly realized two things: "One, he's smarter than you, and, two, he's meaner than a junkyard dog."

He transferred this mode of operation to the Senate, where the Gramm-Rudman-Hollings Deficit Reduction Act soon proved that his audacity had survived the move from the House. Gramm had not been in the Senate a year when he floated the deficit-reduction proposal. He proposed it as a free-standing amendment to the 1985 debt-ceiling legislation.

As in his handling of the Reagan budgets in the House, he sought out two lawmakers, Republican Warren B. Rudman of New Hampshire and Democrat Ernest F. Hollings of South Carolina, who did much to add credibility to his proposal and buffer the ill feeling toward Gramm shared by many senators.

One of Gramm's detractors was then-senator Gary Hart, D-Colo., who referred to the Texan's earlier behavior in the House as a "plot to break the back of the federal government with a sneak attack" and added: "I smell a rat."

Even Dole, who was in his first year as Senate majority leader, seemed less than pleased with Gramm's budget-cutting bill. At one point, Dole urged a swift vote on Gramm-Rudman, warning

Interest Group Ratings

These ratings represent the percentage of votes Phil Gramm cast in agreement with each group's stated position on test votes selected by the groups. The groups are the liberal Americans for Democratic Action, the conservative Americans for Constitutional Action (1979–80), the American Conservative Union, the AFL-CIO and the U.S. Chamber of Commerce.

Year	ADA	ACA/ACU	AFL-CIO	USCC
Senate				
1994	5	100	0	90
1993	5	92	0	100
1992	0	93	8	100
1991	0	95	17	89
1990	0	91	22	92
1989	0	96	0	88
1988	0	95	0	92
1987	5	100	10	89
1986	0	100	0	89
1985	0	95	0	86
House				
1984	10	64	22	78
1983	0	100	0	88
1982	10	91	10	73
1981	0	93	13	89
1980	0	71	11	78
1979	0	77	20	82

that if it sat around too long, "people might start to read it."

But the power of the idea was inescapable, and this one escaped much of the scrutiny usually accorded legislation by the committee process. In the end, even so liberal a Democrat as Edward M. Kennedy of Massachusetts voted for it.

Gramm has illustrated that he is willing to play the inside game. He has demonstrated that he knows how to work through the committee system when it suits him, demonstrating his negotiating skills on banking matters. During the 1990 budget summit, Gramm initially backed the deal, new taxes and all, only to vote against it on the floor.

Still, Sen. Paul Coverdell, R-Ga., observed that he sees Gramm as a "concept legislator not all caught up in having 28 amendments to the ABC bill but rather using the legislature to make clear to the country issues that they have to confront."

Health Care Horatius

Most recently, Gramm showed this flair in his opposition to health care legislation in 1993 and 1994. A number of moderate legislators in both parties bogged down in the minutiae of the Clinton administration bill, or felt compelled to craft a comprehensive substitute. Gramm studied the proposal in detail but eschewed backroom negotiations toward a compromise. Instead, he reduced the administration plan to a few elements he could characterize in terms voters could understand.

"I believe when the American people know that the Clinton plan is good old-fashioned socialized medicine, government running the health care system, they're going to reject it," Gramm said in October 1993.

"He was one of the only ones who could pick up a musket and go fight," said Coverdell. "I was comforted by the speed of that."

While Dole worked diligently behind the scenes to maintain Republican unity, Gramm served primarily as the spokesman for the right-leaning opposition, prodding Dole and the rest of his colleagues toward his stance. Gramm's opposition to the health care bill was indicative of his legislative career in other ways, too. His ability to boil complex subject matter down to simple, telling themes has been one of his most powerful assets. All candidates long to do this, but few succeed as well as Gramm, who has benefited from the arm's length attitude he maintains from the institution he inhabits.

"I have this theory that the closer you are to power the worse you do [as a candidate for another office]," says Ross K. Baker, a professor of political science at Rutgers University. "It makes it difficult to communicate with average voters."

One Certain Little Guy

Gramm has worked hard to craft his appeal to the common man. Since his first days on the floor of the Senate he has spoken of those who "pull the wagon" in America. Whenever he gives a major address—including his announcement speech in February 1995 and his keynote address to the 1992 GOP national convention in Houston—he returns to his oft-told story about a printer from Mexia, Texas, named Dickie Flatt. Gramm says he never votes on a spending or tax bill without stopping to ask how it will affect Flatt.

The folksy style has served Gramm well at home. In his 1990 Senate election, for example, it was part of the reason Gramm could count on rural conservatives as well as suburban voters impressed by his years of hard work and constituent service.

Gramm has yet to test the effectiveness of this Texas formula on a national scale. "I don't think he has the emotional base in the electorate to be a populist," says Buchanan, even though he calls Gramm "an impressive self-promoter" and "the classic political entrepreneur."

Some believe Gramm's Texas persona may prove to be a liability. Lance V. Tarrance Jr., a senior adviser to Alexander, argues that Texas is an important marker in American politics that can help or hurt. Tarrance notes that many Americans could find the culture of Texas politics alien and Gramm's language too remote to be comprehensible. Asked Tarrance: "How are you going to pronounce Mexia?"

On closer inspection, observers will find that Gramm's record at home is not without its reversals. While he has been recognized for his key role in energizing and transforming the Texas Republican Party, he has fallen short when it has come to expanding his influence over Texas politics. In the most recent example, during the 1994 race for Texas party chairman, Gramm's candidate, Rep. Joe L. Barton, lost out to Pauken. While both candidates boasted strong conservative credentials, Barton suffered in part because of his Washington ties.

Gramm's critics back home have also raised the issue of his apparent contradictions. A 1993 series of stories in the *Dallas Morning News,* for example, portrayed Gramm not as a burning idealist,

Texans: Rough Road to the White House

As Sen. Phil Gramm pursues the presidency in 1996 he also will be seeking a third term representing Texas in the Senate. He can do both thanks to a Lone Star State statute often called "the LBJ law" for its original beneficiary. Lyndon B. Johnson was the Democratic nominee for vice president in 1960, even as he was seeking re-election in the Senate. Rather than force Johnson to gamble his career on the fortunes of the national ticket, the state legislature obligingly enacted a law to let him run for both offices at once.

Johnson

The same law was relied upon twice by former senator Lloyd Bentsen, who was the Democratic nominee for vice president in 1988 and who made a try for the top spot on the ticket in 1976. In both years, he wound up settling for another term in the Senate. Bentsen received only 6 of the state's 98 delegates in 1976, but he held his Senate seat by handily defeating a young economist from Texas A&M University in the Democratic voting. (The challenger was Gramm, who did not switch to the GOP until 1983.)

Bensten

As a rule, the early delegate-selecting events have not been kind to Texans. Even incumbents have taken their lumps in New Hampshire's first-in-the-nation primary. Johnson stayed out of the event as a candidate in 1960, won it easily as sitting president in 1964 and then suffered humiliation in 1968 when he managed less than 50 percent. George Bush listed himself as a Texan when he ran in New Hampshire in 1980 and lost by a 2–1 ratio to Ronald Reagan. Another Texan did even worse that year; former governor John B. Connally received less than 2 percent of the vote. Bush won the Granite State primary in 1988 (when he was Reagan's sitting vice president and listed himself on the ballot as a resident of neighboring Maine), but he stumbled again when he returned as incumbent president four years later and received a disappointing 53 percent.

but as a cunning and ambitious politician. The series, based on internal campaign memos, confirmed what Gramm's detractors had charged for years—that in Texas he brazenly abandons the budget-cutting image he cultivates in Washington. The story concluded that aides recommended "deception and illusion" in creating "scores of taxpayer-paid media events for the Texas Republican and his wife, Wendy."

Even some Texans wonder whether Gramm is the right candidate for the party to put up against Clinton. "If you're going to grab the moral high ground, you better be able to stand on the moral high ground," said Stephen P. Munisteri, a Houston businessman who is supporting Alexander.

The Next Level

Interestingly, many of the same questions that were first asked about Gramm as an upstart freshman senator are now being asked about him as a presidential candidate.

"I think what Gramm has to worry about is something that Bob Dole has had to struggle with, [which is] not always being a nice guy," Munisteri said. "His persona comes across as gruff and abrasive."

Many of his closest supporters acknowledge that Gramm has yet to show the polish of a presidential contender. During a March 1 appearance on "Larry King Live," when asked if he would choose a female running mate, he quipped, "Sophia Loren is not a citizen."

At the same time, Gramm's forthrightness could be the very quality the voters are hungriest for after four years of a Clinton administration dogged by public uncertainty about its vision for the nation.

"In a sense, Bill Clinton personally was the catalyst of anxiety and free-flowing concern that have been out there for a long time," Baker said of the 1994 election. "It seems to me inescapable that this unhappiness with Clinton got transferred. And I think that Gramm understands that one of the things that people find lacking in Bill Clinton is resolution."

If the electorate's desire for a well-defined mind and a resolute manner in the White House makes an argument for Gramm's can-

Phil Gramm bills himself as the candidate most committed to shaking up the federal establishment.

didacy, it will also sharpen the questions about Gramm's claim to those qualities. Gramm can portray himself as the one contender who has the least self-doubt and the fewest qualms, but his self-assurance does not guarantee that the inherent conflicts within his political identity, like those of any other politician, will not come forth to embarrass or cripple him at an inopportune time.

"I think that everyone of the candidates has a learning curve," said Gramm campaign adviser Francis. "Part of what this campaign is about is how the candidates grow and mature. Phil Gramm's career has always been about getting to the next level."

Gramm has unquestionably grown and matured in the course of his political career to date. The sheer force of his drive to excel should not be underestimated, however daunting its next target. At the same time, however, the presidency is more than just "the next level" in American politics. Seeking the Oval Office presents a wholly different challenge that imposes distinct demands on an individual.

In coming this close to his party's nomination, Gramm has traveled as far from his origins and expectations as any previous presidential contender, but the figurative last mile to the White House has always proven the most difficult.

Richard Lugar

Serious, disciplined, thoughtful and deliberate, Sen. Richard G. Lugar, R-Ind., hardly seems the gambling kind. Yet his campaign for the Republican presidential nomination is based on a pure hunch, one not supported by the recent history of White House campaigning: Lugar is betting that he can get people to vote for him even though quite often he is telling them things they don't want to hear.

Lugar flouts the conventional wisdom by talking down farm subsidies in Iowa, talking up sales taxes in New Hampshire and preaching an active U.S. role in foreign affairs wherever he goes.

Lugar officially announced for president back home in Indiana on April 19, 1995, a date that turned out to be awful in terms of gaining media exposure for his campaign launch. The same morning in Oklahoma City, a bomb blast ripped into the Alfred P. Murrah Federal Building, an event that captivated the media and the country for days afterward.

Polls suggest he has yet to move since that beginning, remaining near the bottom of the GOP field in popular support. Yet Lugar has forged on, ever methodical and determined, making the rounds in Iowa and New Hampshire, appearing on CNN's "Larry King Live" and other national TV public affairs programs, building an organization and raising money.

"I've always been a long-distance runner," he said in announcing. At the end of June, Lugar's campaign reported that it had topped the $3 million mark in fund-raising. That was a respectable sum, considering that by the end of March Lugar had collected barely over $500,000, but Lugar's midyear total was less than one-fourth of that

Richard G. Lugar

Republican of Indianapolis, Ind.
Born: April 4, 1932, Indianapolis, Ind.
Education: Denison University, B.A. 1954; Oxford University, B.A. 1956, M.A. 1956.
Family: Wife, Charlene Smeltzer; four children.
Religion: Methodist.
Political career: Indianapolis School Board, 1964–67; mayor of Indianapolis, 1968–75; Republican nominee for U.S. Senate, 1974; U.S. Senate, 1977–present.
Occupation: Manufacturing executive; farm manager.
Military service: Navy, 1957–60.

amassed by Sens. Bob Dole of Kansas or Phil Gramm of Texas, who are, respectively, the front-runner and chief chaser in the GOP field.

Media pundits generally have had kind words for Lugar. In *Newsweek,* George Will wrote that Lugar's "conspicuous normality and undeniable gravitas certainly improve the Republican field." The *Wall Street Journal's* Albert R. Hunt praised his "character and capacity." But in the same breath, most analysts have discounted Lugar's chances of winning the nomination. "He sounds reasoned and reasonable about national issues," newsletter publisher Stuart Rothenberg wrote, "but he doesn't excite people, isn't in the same league as Dole and Gramm in terms of money, and doesn't have a niche in the party."

In officially announcing his bid, Lugar anticipated this kiss of death and sought to parry what he called "the conventional wisdom of generous columnists." Lugar predicted the pundits would say he "is intelligent, has broad experience, [and] exercises courage and prudence appropriately." But Lugar also predicted the judgment "that such a person is rarely nominated or elected."

This analysis, the candidate argued that day, underestimates "the wisdom of the American people" who "know that the presidency is not entertainment" and will respond to a candidacy that offers "straight talk and serious action."

Lugar's "straight and serious" formula begins with foreign policy. He plays up his foreign policy expertise and stresses that as president he would define a broad and assertive role for America in the post-Cold War world.

That includes the thankless theater of the Balkans. To quell the fighting in Bosnia and force the Serbs into a diplomatic settlement, Lugar called for sending a "robust, heavily armed" NATO force of 70,000 troops, up to one-third of them American. He did so long before November 1995, when President Clinton engineered a Bosnia peace agreement and committed 20,000 U.S. troops to a NATO force.

Among GOP presidential hopefuls, Lugar was alone in advocating such a "bold course" solution in Bosnia, which he said was necessary in order to safeguard European security "as well as our own."

This same sort of "do the right thing" mentality emerges when Lugar turns to his other area of special preparation: agriculture.

From his pulpit as Senate Agriculture Committee chairman, Lugar has proposed phasing down the federal government's agriculture subsidy programs. He has done so despite his roots in Indiana, where he still owns a farm. And he has done so despite the importance of Iowa, site of the first delegate-selecting caucuses in the presidential nominating process, where many farmers derive substantial income from federal subsidies.

Here again, Lugar argues the greatest good in the long run. Getting rid of subsidies, he says, would enhance farmers' incomes by encouraging them to grow crops for lucrative overseas markets instead of relying on government subsidies.

By the same token, Lugar has not trimmed his sails for New Hampshire, home of the first primary and a do-or-die stop for a dark-horse GOP contender. The New Hampshire state GOP is strongly influenced by opponents of gun control. Yet Lugar in the 103rd Congress supported a five-day waiting period for handgun purchases and a ban on certain assault-style weapons.

And, as if he needed additional controversy in New Hampshire and elsewhere, Lugar has been explaining how radically he wants to restructure the way taxes are collected.

Lugar loses no Republicans by arguing that the federal income

How Lugar Voted . . .

Congressional Quarterly each year selects a series of key votes on major issues and records how every member voted on each. The following examples were culled from Lugar's 19 years in the Senate.

1995 Allow vote on Henry W. Foster Jr. as surgeon general   N
Approve balanced-budget constitutional amendment   Y
Approve budget resolution eliminating deficit by 2002   Y
1994 Safeguard access to abortion clinics   N
Bar military action in Haiti without vote in Congress   Y
End U.S. arms embargo on Bosnia   Y
Approve national education standards   N
End U.S. trade embargo on Vietnam   N
1993 Require unpaid family and medical leave   N
Provide incentives to limit campaign spending   N
Pass Clinton budget with new taxes and cuts   N
Authorize funds for the National Service program   N
Confirm Ruth Bader Ginsburg to the Supreme Court   Y
Reduce spending for anti-missile program   N
Provide foreign aid to Russia   Y
Allow federal abortion funding   N
Cut military funds in Somalia after troop withdrawal   Y
Ban certain semiautomatic assault weapons   Y
Approve national "motor voter" registration bill   N
Approve five-day waiting period to buy handguns   Y
Approve NAFTA   Y
Approve budget increasing taxes and reducing deficit   N
Support president's right to lift military gay ban   N
1992 Provide extended unemployment benefits   Y
Oppose deeper cuts in spending for SDI   Y
Impose nine-month ban on nuclear testing   N
Reduce enterprise zones and IRA deductions   Y
Allow abortion counseling at federally funded clinics   Y
Provide $26.5 billion for foreign assistance   Y
Approve school-choice pilot program   Y
Allow funds shift from defense to domestic programs   N
Reject lifting fetal tissue research ban   Y

... On the Major Issues

1991	Approve waiting period for handgun purchases	Y
	Appropriate $509 million for super collider	N
	Raise senators' pay and ban honoraria	Y
	Tie China's trade status to human rights progress	N
	Provide up to 20 more weeks of jobless benefits	N
	Pass Civil Rights Act of 1991	Y
1990	Oppose ban on some semiautomatic weapons	Y
	Adopt constitutional amendment on flag desecration	Y
	Oppose requiring parental notice for minors' abortion	N
	Halt production of B-2 stealth bomber at 13 planes	N
1989	Oppose reduction of SDI funding	Y
	Oppose barring federal funds for "obscene" art	Y
1988	Approve death penalty for drug-related murders	Y
	Oppose workfare amendment to welfare overhaul bill	N
1987	Limit testing of anti-ballistic missiles in space	N
	Confirm Supreme Court nominee Robert H. Bork	Y
1986	Impose sanctions on South Africa	Y
	Amend Constitution to require a balanced budget	Y
1985	Weaken gun control laws	Y
	Reject school prayer	Y
1984	Retain funds for SDI or "star wars" research	Y
	Permit school prayer	Y
1983	Overturn Supreme Court ruling legalizing abortion	Y
	Create Martin Luther King Jr. holiday	Y
1982	Cut $1.2 billion for public works jobs	Y
	Retain tobacco price supports	N
1981	Disapprove sale of AWACS planes to Saudi Arabia	N
	Index income tax rates against inflation	Y
1980	Approve military draft legislation	Y
	End revenue sharing to the states	N
1979	Kill stronger windfall profits tax on oil companies	Y
	Impose moratorium on nuclear power plant building	N
1978	Approve treaty giving Panama Canal to Panama	N
	Approve airline deregulation bill	Y
1977	End federal price controls for onshore natural gas	Y
	Kill cap on outside income at 15 percent of Senate pay	N

tax discourages savings, investment and productivity, nor by advocating that tax's abolition (along with the Internal Revenue Service). But he also proposes replacing the income tax with a national sales tax—a novel concept to most Americans and one that many view as a scheme to let Uncle Sam reach deeper into their pockets.

Lugar's willingness to tackle these issues can be called courage or a chin-first approach to politics. Either way, its origins can be glimpsed in his political education.

Lugar was born in 1932, in the city that later would be the springboard to his career in national politics, Indianapolis. The Hoosier state was a model of competitive, two-party politics during Lugar's growing-up years; Indiana elected both Democratic and Republican governors and senators, and it voted two times Democratic and three times Republican for president before Lugar headed east (toward Granville, Ohio) to attend Denison University.

He graduated in 1954, was named a Rhodes scholar and took a degree from Oxford University in 1956, the same year he married Charlene Smeltzer. While in England, Lugar enlisted in the Navy. Today, in one of the rare hardballs he throws at President Clinton on the presidential trail, Lugar contrasts himself to his fellow Rhodes scholar who never served in the military.

"Americans will rest easier," Lugar has said, "in the knowledge that the president standing watch over our country's safety and security is someone who actually knows what it means to stand a watch." Lugar served in the Navy as a briefing officer on intelligence matters, making a reputation for himself in the Pentagon. He returned home in 1960 and got involved in running the family tool business and livestock and grain operation. A product of Indianapolis public schools and eventually a father of four, he won his first election in 1964, to the Indianapolis School Board.

Three years later, he took over the mayor's office by beating incumbent Democrat John Barton. Lugar's conservative, efficient mayoral administration won him favorable notices all over Indiana and well beyond. Mayor Lugar was a spokesman for Nixon administration policies, and he came to be known as "Richard Nixon's favorite mayor."

The Nixon connection was a dead weight for Lugar in the Watergate election year of 1974, when he challenged two-term Democ-

Lugar's Proving Ground

Sen. Richard G. Lugar took an unusual route to national politics: local politics. Lugar's small pond was Indianapolis, where he first served on the school board in 1964 and became mayor by ousting an incumbent Democrat in 1967.

As mayor, Lugar transformed the jurisdiction. In 1970, he pushed through an innovative plan to consolidate the city (the state capital) and nearby communities of Marion County under one government.

The plan, dubbed Unigov, consolidated such functions as zoning, planning, health care, park maintenance and capital improvements on a countywide basis, while maintaining separate school and police districts.

Unigov increased the city's population by about 250,000 and its geographic size by 275 square miles, propelling Indianapolis into the top echelon of cities, from No. 25 in population in 1968 to No. 12 in 1975. That leap made it possible to build modern sports facilities and attract major league teams and national conventions.

Even the initial critics came to appreciate Unigov, which unified community politics and slowed flight to the suburbs.

Unigov secured the reputation that Lugar had already established as one of the most effective mayors in the United States. His knowledge of urban affairs and his political pragmatism had appealed to delegates at the 1969 National League of Cities, where he beat New York Mayor John V. Lindsay in a race for the organization's vice presidency (and put himself in line to be its next president).

President Richard M. Nixon took notice of the straight-shooting conservative who had been willing to speak up for the White House and oppose big-city Democratic mayors. Lugar became a keynote speaker at the 1972 GOP convention and was appointed to the Advisory Commission on Intergovernmental Relations. A *Washington Post* reporter tagged Lugar "Nixon's favorite mayor"—a sobriquet that Lugar would spend years trying to shed.

In 1974, the year Nixon resigned in the wake of Watergate, Lugar failed in his first bid for statewide office, losing a Senate race to Democratic incumbent Birch Bayh. But in that disastrous season for Republicans, Lugar ran well enough to be the acknowledged party champion two years later against the weaker Democratic incumbent, Sen. Vance Hartke.

ratic senator Birch Bayh. Lugar got a solid 46 percent of the vote in defeat, and two years later, taking on three-term Democratic senator Vance Hartke, he got 59 percent. The recession of 1982 trimmed Lugar to 54 percent against Democratic Rep. Floyd Fithian, but his 1988 and 1994 campaigns were walkaways. The most recent victory made him the first Indiana senator to be elected to a fourth term.

Early in his Senate career, Lugar established a reputation as a hard worker; conservative, but not orthodox, and non-ideological in mien; a listener looking to build bridges to achieve his legislative goals. Lugar's first major job came in 1978, when he and Utah Republican Orrin G. Hatch teamed to lead a successful filibuster against a package of labor law changes strongly pushed by the AFL-CIO.

Also in 1978, he supported legislation providing federal aid to financially strapped New York City, and in 1979, he played a role in passing a measure rescuing the Chrysler Corp. from bankruptcy; only Michigan had more Chrysler employees than Indiana. Lugar was responsible for a provision of the bailout bill requiring Chrysler's unions to make a pay concession to help return the company to solvency.

Lugar's first experience waging a presidential campaign came in 1979, when he managed the bid of his close ally in the Senate, Republican leader Howard H. Baker Jr. The Tennesseean's bid never took wing, and his effort folded in early 1980.

A sign of Lugar's growing prominence and popularity in the Senate came in 1983, when he defeated incumbent Republican Bob Packwood for the job of chairing the National Republican Senatorial Committee for the 1984 campaign cycle. Lugar raised record amounts of money for GOP candidates, and Republicans sighed in relief when their net loss in the Senate was just two seats, keeping them in the majority.

After the election, Lugar entered the contest to succeed Baker as majority leader (Baker had not sought re-election in 1984). But Baker's easygoing stewardship left many GOP senators longing for more discipline in the chamber, and Lugar's personality was not that of a whip-cracker. Among five candidates, he ran third, and he dropped out after the third ballot, on which he drew 13 votes. (There were 20 each for Ted Stevens of Alaska and for Dole, the eventual winner.)

Senate Candidacies

Election	Votes	Percentage
1994 General		
Lugar (R)	1,039,625	67.4
J. Jontz (D)	470,799	30.5
B. Bourland (Libertarian)	17,343	1.1
Mary C. Barton (New Alliance)	15,801	1.0
1988 General		
Lugar (R)	1,430,525	68.0
Jack Wickes (D)	668,778	32.0
1982 General		
Lugar (R)	978,301	54.0
Floyd Fithian (D)	828,400	46.0
1976 General		
Lugar (R)	1,275,833	59.0
Vance Hartke (D)	878,522	41.0

Lugar's consolation prize was the chairmanship of the Foreign Relations Committee, and he performed so impressively in that post that at times in the 99th Congress (1985–87) he seemed to function as a kind of shadow secretary of state.

Early in 1986, President Ronald Reagan asked Lugar to head a U.S. delegation monitoring the Philippines election between Ferdinand Marcos and challenger Corazon Aquino. Lugar quickly concluded that Marcos was stealing the election. Privately he implored Reagan to denounce Marcos, but Reagan argued instead that there had been fraud on both sides.

Lugar persisted. Eventually the administration pressured Marcos to leave office peacefully, in what came to be regarded as one of Reagan's chief foreign policy achievements. But in 1989, Aquino gave the credit to Lugar. "Without him," she said, "there would be no Philippine-U.S. relations to speak of by now."

Also in the 99th Congress, Lugar pressed the Reagan administration to accommodate the overwhelming sentiment in Congress

CQ Vote Studies

Participation: The percentage of recorded votes for which Richard Lugar was present and voting.

Presidential Support: The percentage of votes on which Lugar agreed with the public position of the president.

Party Unity: The percentage of votes on which Lugar agreed with a majority of Democrats (1979–82) or Republicans (1983-present) voting against a majority of the opposing party.

Conservative Coalition: The percentage of votes on which Lugar stood with a majority of Republicans and Southern Democrats against a majority of Northern Democrats.

Year	Voting Participation	Presidential Support		Party Unity		Conservative Coalition	
		S	O	S	O	S	O
1994	100	45	55	78	22	78	22
1993	99	34	65	88	12	88	10
1992	97	87	10	86	12	76	21
1991	98	93	7	88	11	83	10
1990	99	86	11	86	12	97	3
1989	97	93	2	83	15	89	11
1988	95	86	13	76	19	86	14
1987	95	76	21	77	20	78	13
1986	99	88	11	89	10	88	9
1985	99	89	10	92	8	88	12
1984	100	92	8	94	6	87	13
1983	100	95	5	92	8	95	5
1982	98	83	15	85	14	84	16
1981	99	90	9	93	7	90	10
1980	93	44	53	80	12	85	10
1979	99	43	57	90	10	90	10
1978	99	35	64	85	14	80	20
1977	98	48	51	91	8	95	4

Note: S–supported; O–opposed.

to impose economic penalties against South Africa's apartheid government. Reagan eventually responded with mild penalties, but when Democrats threatened to take control of the issue with their proposal for harsher sanctions, Lugar stepped in with his own sanctions bill. His efforts at compromise succeeded, even though Reagan never embraced them and Jesse Helms, R-N.C., opposed them.

After the Democrats captured a Senate majority in the 1986 election, Lugar lost not only his chairmanship on Foreign Relations, but the ranking seat as well. Lugar had moved into the chair in the 99th Congress because the more senior Helms had wanted to lead the Agriculture Committee. But for the 100th, Helms reasserted his claim to Foreign Relations, and by a vote of 24–17, the Republican Conference supported his right to bump Lugar.

Another career disappointment for Lugar came in August 1988, when George Bush chose as his vice presidential running mate Dan Quayle, Lugar's junior Indiana colleague in Senate years and influence. Lugar had been on most people's lists of vice presidential prospects in 1988, as he had been in 1980. But suddenly, it was Quayle on the national stage, greatly complicating Lugar's hopes of seeking national office. Lugar's entry into the current GOP contest came after Quayle announced in February 1995 that he would not try for the 1996 nomination.

Although displaced by Helms from his formal role as the top Senate Republican on Foreign Affairs, Lugar has continued to function as a prominent party spokesman on foreign policy. That is partly because Helms' role as a conservative polemicist often puts him at odds with other Republicans (he got along especially poorly with the Bush White House), and partly because Helms, unlike Lugar, has frosty relations with the media.

Lugar enjoyed national notice (and international importance) during the Persian Gulf crisis of 1990–91. He took the lead among Foreign Relations Republicans on the U.S. response to the August 1990 occupation of Kuwait by forces of Iraqi President Saddam Hussein. After the invasion, Lugar raced out ahead of Bush, whose stated goal was simply to get Iraq to give up Kuwait. "It seems to me important that Saddam Hussein must either leave or be removed," Lugar said.

Lugar also insisted Congress needed to fulfill what he viewed as its constitutional responsibility to authorize the use of military

Interest Group Ratings

These ratings represent the percentage of votes Richard Lugar cast in agreement with each group's stated position on test votes selected by the groups. The groups are the liberal Americans for Democratic Action, the conservative Americans for Constitutional Action (1977–80), the American Conservative Union (1981–94), the AFL-CIO and the U.S. Chamber of Commerce (1977–94).

Year	ADA	ACA/ACU	AFL-CIO	USCC
1994	10	76	0	90
1993	10	72	0	100
1992	10	85	17	100
1991	10	76	17	90
1990	6	83	11	75
1989	10	75	0	100
1988	10	88	21	92
1987	5	72	20	88
1986	10	78	0	89
1985	5	74	10	90
1984	10	82	18	79
1983	15	44	12	68
1982	15	63	28	70
1981	5	100	0	94
1980	17	83	11	86
1979	11	89	0	100
1978	10	92	11	89
1977	10	81	10	94

force. Even before the 101st Congress adjourned in late October 1990, Lugar said, "Congress ought to come back into session to entertain a declaration of war."

Still, Lugar emerged as a Senate point man for Bush's gulf policy. Lugar spoke frequently, in the Senate and during national television interviews, in favor of the January 1991 resolution authorizing military force.

Despite the U.S.-led military rout that liberated Kuwait, Lugar's hopes for Saddam's immediate downfall were not met; instead, the Iraqi strongman used what military might he had left to crush revolts among his nation's Kurdish and Shiite Muslim populations. Lugar nonetheless defended Bush against criticism that he had stopped short of Saddam's removal and had reacted slowly to the plight of Iraq's minority groups.

Since the Cold War's end, Lugar has been an influential advocate of the view that the United States should act vigorously and give aid generously to save the republics of the former Soviet Union from economic collapse. He stands foursquare for expanding NATO into former Eastern bloc territory and has criticized the Clinton administration for laxity in consulting with Congress and educating the public on the matter.

Similarly, he pushed Clinton to force a broader public dialogue on the war in Bosnia by seeking congressional authority for the use of U.S. military force in the Balkans.

Back to the Farms

When Lugar was knocked out of the top GOP seat on Foreign Relations in 1987, he moved into the ranking seat on the Agriculture Committee, where he forged a close working relationship with Democratic Chairman Patrick J. Leahy of Vermont. Their cooperation continues in the 104th Congress, with Lugar now in the chair and Leahy as ranking.

Both Lugar and Leahy have been strong advocates of downsizing the Agriculture Department bureaucracy, paring down the extensive federal price support system and focusing more attention on farming methods that protect the environment.

Lugar's environmentalist tendencies are stronger than those of most Senate Republicans, and of many Agriculture Committee members of either party. He worked with Leahy to block changes sought by farm organizations in environmental restrictions in the 1985 farm bill, including the "swampbuster" provisions requiring cutoffs in federal payments to farmers who drain protected wetlands.

With congressional Republicans scouring every line of the current budget to find ways to save money for tax cuts as well as for deficit reduction, Lugar is pressing his plan to gradually but significantly cut back the multibillion-dollar web of farm subsidy programs. He wants to reduce crop target prices by 3 percent a year for the next five years, an approach that would ultimately put target prices just above likely market prices. Because subsidies to farmers are based on the gap between those two prices, the federal government would save billions of dollars. Lugar also wants to eliminate the Export Enhancement Program, which helps U.S. farmers compete overseas by subsidizing commodity exports.

Opponents of the cuts essentially accuse Lugar of parochialism: They say his Indiana farmers enjoy good soil, moderate weather, predictable yields and the option of growing a diverse range of crops. They do not need the safety net of federal price supports as farmers do in the Great Plains, where conditions are less favorable.

Undeterred by such criticism, Lugar presses his case on the presidential trail, even in Iowa, where hardscrabble corn growers in the less fertile western part of the state are among the farmers who would have the toughest time adjusting to a world without price supports.

Indianapolis Star reporter Mary Beth Schneider wrote in June 1995 that while his candor is "refreshing," voters "don't seem to elect the leadership they claim to want. Candidates who offer tough solutions to tough problems lose to candidates who say we can have it all and it won't cost us a thing."

Lugar respectfully dissents from this conclusion. In the first months of 1996, he will have his chance to disprove it.

Other Candidates

Third-Party Candidates

While they fight each other for the presidency in 1996, the two major parties will also be fighting another battle, in which their interests coincide —a battle to maintain their joint control of the American political process. How they manage this second challenge may be just as important in the long run as who wins the presidency in 1996.

American politics has been a story of two-party domination. In the beginning, there were the Federalists and the Jeffersonian Democrats. They were followed by the Whigs and Jacksonian Democrats. Since the 1850s, the two teams have been known as Republicans and Democrats.

After two centuries, that two-party domination has shown signs of weakening. Twenty percent of the ballots in the 1992 presidential election were withheld from the major parties (19 percent went for independent Ross Perot, nearly 1 percent for a collection of third parties, led by the Libertarians). Perot's vote was remarkably consistent across all regions of the country, but because it was not concentrated in certain strongholds, he won no states and therefore no Electoral College votes. He did not even win a single congressional district.

Still, the Texas billionaire led a defection from the two major parties that was the second largest since the Civil War, surpassed only by the 35 percent that went for an array of third parties in 1912. That year, the assault on the two-party system was led by former president Theodore Roosevelt's Progressive Party.

Perot's movement is unusual in that it survived the presidential cycle. In the past, major disaffection with the two parties has been short-lived. Significant third parties have been like shooting stars, brilliant but brief. Their supporters are usually reabsorbed into the two-party system by the next election.

Before Perot, all the major independent or third-party candidates this century—Roosevelt in 1912, Robert M. La Follette in 1924, George C. Wallace in 1968 and John B. Anderson in 1980—had either died, retired from the political scene or gone back to their original party by the time of the next presidential election.

There are signs that 1996 may break dramatically from this pattern. Perot continues to demand attention, both as a prospective candidate and as the source of support for a third party. Moreover, one of the candidates some Republicans wanted to lure into their primary contests, retired Army general Colin L. Powell, was thought to have the ability to affect the outcome unpredictably by running as an independent.

Moreover, politicians from Jesse Jackson to former Connecticut governor Lowell P. Weicker Jr. have mentioned the possibility of mounting independent candidacies themselves in 1996. So has retiring Democratic senator Bill Bradley of New Jersey, who, like Jackson, has expressed interest in an independent bid rather than a challenge to President Clinton in the Democratic primaries.

Some see commentator Patrick J. Buchanan leading an independent movement on the right in 1996 if he loses in the primaries and the Republican nomination goes to someone he considers too liberal on abortion. Elements of the populist left have talked of drafting former California governor Edmund G. "Jerry" Brown Jr. in 1996, despite his apparent lack of interest so far in this cycle. Brown has run three times in the Democratic primaries.

Historical Circumstances

The attractiveness of the independent route for the 1996 cycle reflects the power of incumbency in the presidential nominating process. No matter how much any Democrat may want the nomination, the fact remains that President Bill Clinton will almost certainly get it. No president in this century who sought another term has been denied renomination by his party. Clinton, despite an approval rating that had only occasionally been above 50 percent in most opinion polls, approached the last year of his term with a commanding lead in funds and commitments.

Still, the interest shown by Jackson and Bradley also reflects a political climate that is increasingly restive and dissatisfied with the candidates and policy choices put forward by the major parties. Weicker has already tapped that mood on the state level. In 1990 he won election as governor of Connecticut as an independent (he did not run for a second term in 1994).

According to Everett Carll Ladd, the president of the Roper Center for Public Opinion Research at the University of Connecticut, public sentiment for alternatives to the two major parties has been fueled by a powerful confluence of events. Americans always have had a relatively weak party system, says Ladd, and it has grown even weaker in the television age. The electorate is less and less likely to express a distinct partisan identification. The media are increasingly critical of centralized authority.

Ladd says these trends have been demonstrated recently not only in the support for Perot's candidacy in 1992 but also in the nationwide movement in support of term limits. (Term limits for members of Congress have been adopted in each of the 23 states where they have been put to a vote, although the Supreme Court on May 22, 1995, declared such limits unconstitutional.)

Many voters are unlikely to be mollified by the alternatives that the major parties are expected to offer in 1996, Ladd says. "The weakness of Clinton. The weakness of [Kansas Republican Sen. Bob] Dole. The weakness of everyone else adds to the other factors."

Overcoming Obstacles

Still, those who dream of breaking generations of political precedent must produce answers to several daunting questions. A third-option candidate must replace the organization and money that usually accrue to major-party nominees by virtue of their nominations.

Perot was able to level the playing field in 1992 by spending about $63 million out of his own pocket. For candidates who lack such a fortune, the fund-raising process can be slow and difficult. Contributions from individuals cannot exceed $1,000; contributions from political action committees cannot exceed $5,000. If, unlike Perot in 1992, a candidate chooses to accept public financing, he cannot contribute more than $50,000 of his own money to his presidential campaign. Even then, a candidate can receive public money only after the election and then only by winning at least 5 percent of the nationwide popular vote. The amount of public money he would collect would be tied to his share of the vote.

Even well-financed independent candidates such as Perot must divert much of their time and money to gaining a spot on the ballot. It is an intricate process with deadlines and petition requirements that vary from state to state.

Richard Winger, the publisher of *Ballot Access News,* says a candidate seeking to run nationwide in 1996 would need to collect at a minimum an aggregate of nearly 700,000 signatures to get on the ballot nationwide as an independent. A candidate interested in forming a new third party would need to gather even more signatures to meet the requirements of some states.

History of the Challenge

In the past, the preferred method of challenging the major parties was to create a full-blown third party. Roosevelt did so in 1912 with the Progressive Party (popularly known as the Bull Moose Party), which elected roughly a dozen members to Congress that year.

In recent times, major challenges to the two major parties have been made by independents. The American Independent Party was almost exclusively a vehicle for Wallace's presidential candidacy in 1968, and Anderson and Perot made no effort to form third parties during their candidacies.

An independent presidential candidacy is easier to launch than a third party and possibly better reflects an electorate dissatisfied with most large political institutions. There are several small third parties that are positioning themselves to tap the mood for change in 1996. According to Winger, the Libertarian Party will be holding its nominating convention in July, culminating a nominating process that will feature presidential primaries in nearly a dozen states. The U.S. Taxpayers Party, which ran Howard Phillips (the longtime head of the Conservative Caucus) for president in 1992, has scheduled its convention for San Diego in August, immediately after the close of the Republican National Convention there.

Disaffected Center

Much of the disaffection with the two parties in the mid-1990s arises not from the extremes of the left-right continuum but from the center. It has not always been this way. Most significant third parties of the past championed a particular cause and had a base of support largely limited to a specific region.

America's first significant third party in the early 19th century, the Anti-Masons, emerged in the Northeast. The agrarian Populist Party of the late 19th century was a powerful force that grew up almost exclusively west of the Mississippi River. The states' rights campaigns of Strom Thurmond in 1948 and Wallace in 1968 showed little pull beyond their home base in the South.

The recent independent candidacies of Anderson and Perot were more national in their appeal. Both men spoke to voters in the center of the political spectrum by stressing the need for more honest and efficient government.

The disaffected middle has grown larger as the years have passed. Anderson peaked at about 25 percent in a Gallup Poll in June 1980 before slumping to 6.6 percent on Election Day as his campaign ran low on money. Perot reached 35 percent in presidential trial heats in the spring of 1992 and finished with 19 percent after exiting and re-entering the presidential race. What was most remarkable about Perot was not the degree to which he faded in the late fall, but the degree to which he sustained his hold.

Previous third-party candidacies had tended to lose altitude as Election Day neared, deflated by massive defections by voters who did not want to waste their vote on a candidate who had no chance of winning. While it was clear during the final days of the 1992 campaign that Perot could not win, his support actually increased. The final pre-election surveys by most of the major polling organizations undervalued Perot's actual Election Day showing by 2 to 5 percentage points.

Part of his late surge was due, no doubt, to the millions of dollars that Perot threw into a fall media blitz—money that previous third-party candidates did not have. It also reflected the willingness of many voters to suspend the normal political practice of limiting their choice to the Democratic or Republican nominees.

Even more voters appear ready to consider options beyond the two major parties in 1996, making it quite possible that there could be a three, four or even five-way race for the White House. If that happens, it would signal something significant unfolding within the American political system beyond the Democrats' and Republicans' control. The only previous time that the two parties lost even 10 percent of the presidential vote in back-to-back elections was in 1856 and 1860, on the eve of the Civil War. That was a period of great political turbulence that featured the demise of one major party (the Whigs) and the birth of another (the Republicans).

Such a striking result is hard to imagine in the late 1990s. Still, the decade has already seen political upheavals that few would have predicted. After the election of a Democratic president in 1992 and a Republican Congress in 1994, voters may not be finished rearranging the political landscape.

The Peristence of Perot

In August 1995, Perot presided over a convention of United We Stand, America—the organization spawned by his candidacy in 1992. The event drew thousands of participants to Dallas, where they were wooed by various presidential candidates eager for the group's support.

The following month, Perot suddenly announced he would launch a third party for the purpose of nominating a candidate for the White House in 1996. While he insisted that he would prefer not to run himself, it was his name and resources that gave the new group instant viability nationwide. At the time, he said: "The most constructive thing for our country is to revitalize the two major parties."

Some saw his latest turnaround as a self-serving attempt to regain a share of the limelight lost in the national fascination with the prospective candidacy of Powell, but Perot insisted the time was ripe for a new third party aimed at the millions of disaffected voters. Citing a recent poll that showed that 62 percent of Americans favored formation of a new party, Perot said, "This is a party for that 62 per cent."

Ross Perot on Election Night 1992

Perot said the new organization would be called the Independence Party. In states such as California, where another party is already using a variation of that name, it will be called the Reform Party. Perot enthusiasts qualified for ballot status under that name in California, Ohio and Maine before the end of 1995.

An actual Perot candidacy remained highly uncertain. While Republicans denounced the idea as a boon to President Clinton's re-election, pollsters pointed out that Perot was far from achieving any role beyond that of spoiler. Perot's standing in the polls had not recovered from his high-profile defeat in opposing the North American Free Trade Agreement in 1993. He still drew about one-fifth of the national vote in some three-way tests, but the number of respondents indicating they would not consider voting for him suggested he would have trouble expanding his base much further.

The Powell Phenomenon

Long the subject of political speculation, Powell burst into stardom in mid-1995 with the publication of his autobiography, *My American Journey,* and a subsequent book tour that generated enormous media coverage. Observers in both parties and throughout the political community noted that Powell's unusual combination

Colin L. Powell

of assets made him a political phenomenon without precedent.

A Persian Gulf war hero widely admired for his calm confidence as well as his exemplary Army career, Powell is also an African-American whose appeal transcends racial and political boundaries. As chairman of the Joint Chiefs of Staff from 1989 to 1993, Powell was the nation's top uniformed officer. He inspired fervent interest in the news media and among voters who regarded him as head-and-shoulders above the current lineup of candidates.

"He offers trust," said historian Stephen E. Ambrose, who helped launch Citizens for Colin Powell, when asked why he and so many were willing to bet on an untested commodity. "I think he has the most admired character in America."

Until his official announcement November 8, 1995, that he would not be a candidate for any elective office in 1996, Powell was regarded as a strong third-party candidate. While he never stated a party preference, spoke out on issues, raised campaign money or put together an organization, he also did not discourage the steady stream of speculation or the efforts of supporters who had been trying to recruit him. For example, during a speech in San Diego in August, Powell said, "There are one or two titles that are better than chairman of the Joint Chiefs of Staff."

With Powell out of the 1996 race, the question of how well Powell would perform in the vastly different world of national politics remains unanswered. "It's a very different job, being a famous military leader and being president," warned House Speaker Newt Gingrich, R-Ga.

A Lane for Jackson?

Civil rights activist Jesse Jackson, a candidate for the Democratic presidential nomination in 1984 and 1988, has said he will not court the party nomination again in 1996—and that is what has the White House worried.

Jesse Jackson

A Jackson candidacy in the spring would not endanger President Clinton's renomination and might even help him position himself for the fall, much as Jackson's hostility helped him do in 1992. But Jackson has threatened to run as an independent in the general election, voicing frustration over what he sees as Clinton's move to the political center. Even an underfinanced Jackson effort would attract enormous support from African-Americans and other constituencies vital to a Democratic victory.

Exit polls in 1992 suggested that one-fifth of Clinton's total vote came from African-Americans. Deprived of this vote, Clinton would lose his slim chance of carrying Southern states other than Arkansas. He would have little chance of carrying the big swing states, such as Illinois, Michigan, Ohio, Pennsylvania and New Jersey.

As of the fall of 1995, most observers had come to believe that Jackson would threaten a campaign without finally launching one. Some saw much of the steam escaping from Jackson's prospective candidacy after Clinton gave a ringing endorsement of affirmative action in July, but if that speech pre-empted one of Jackson's potential themes, he has others—including Clinton's approach to welfare reform and to cuts in federal programs that aid the poor. Not least among Jackson's grievances is the arm's-length treatment he has received from the Clinton White House; Jackson's views on social programs and urban policy have received little attention from the president. "All you can do is give public advice and not private counsel," Jackson has complained.

As a result, Jackson has spoken often of keeping his options open. And he says he does not need to make a final decision until July 1996. In the intervening months, he has promised to monitor Clinton's policy decisions and retire a debt remaining from his 1988 campaign. In September 1995 he announced that arrangements had been made to pay outstanding fines levied against that campaign by the Federal Election Commission, so he could proceed to assess the 1996 questions unencumbered.

Jackson has said that he owes no allegiance to the Democrats. Ronald Walters, a political scientist at Howard University in Washington, D.C., and a strategist for Jackson, pointed out that Jackson's effect on Clinton might be greater as an independent than as a Democrat.

"The independent position will put Jackson in a far stronger position in attempting to extend leverage in the party over public policy issues," Walters said. "He has run a couple of fairly good races [within the party], but when Jackson said, 'Let's talk about issues,' they said, 'Jesse, go sit in a corner'"

That view is shared by some members of the Congressional Black Caucus. It has been noted that a Jackson candidacy, while damaging for Clinton, would probably benefit other Democrats on the ballot by attracting a historic turnout among black voters.

The 1988 race for the Democratic nomination was the high point of Jackson's political career to date. He upset Michael S. Dukakis in the Michigan caucuses, ran all the way to the convention and succeeded in changing the rules for electing delegates to future conventions. Jackson came to the 1988 Democratic National Convention in Atlanta with more than one-fourth of the total number of delegates, enough to force Dukakis to adopt three of Jackson's planks as part of the party platform.

Jackson amassed 400 delegates in 1984, a number that he argued underrepresented the popular vote because he did not reach the 15 percent threshold required to receive delegates in many states.

Bradley at Sea

Expressing discontent with both the Democratic and Republican parties, Bradley announced his retirement from the Senate in August and said he wanted to find a new way to connect Americans to the political process.

Sen. Bill Bradley

While ruling out a primary challenge to Clinton, Bradley left open "an independent route" to the White House. He also spoke of forsaking "the marching band" in which he has played during his political career in favor of "a jazz combo," in which no one knows what will come next.

Bradley, 52, has been mentioned as a future presidential candidate practically since his election to the Senate in 1978. His name has popped up regularly as a presidential contender or as a vice presidential pick since the 1988 cycle.

An All American basketball star at Princeton who won an Olympic gold medal and a Rhodes scholarship, Bradley then played 10 years of professional ball with the New York Knicks. He was elected to the Senate in his first bid for elective office.

Some of the aura that has surrounded his storybook career still persists, although Bradley has not had much to point to since his role in the passage of the 1986 overhaul of the income tax code.

The presidential system is set up on the presumption of a two-party contest. Breaking through the many barriers to independent candidacy would be very difficult for someone with national hero status (such as Powell) or immense wealth and charisma (such as Perot). If Bradley is proposing to penetrate the barriers by virtue of his intelligence and thoughtful manner, his model might well be John B. Anderson, a Republican congressman from Illinois who ran as an independent and received 6.6 percent of the national popular vote in 1980.

"I think it's not very realistic" for an independent to win, said Fred Greenstein, a political scientist at Princeton University and a leading scholar on presidential politics. Bradley might be seen as a respected figure in the Senate, Greenstein said, but he "does not have the fire there" to wage an uphill battle against both parties and the system itself.

In addition to the long odds against success, a Bradley bid in 1996 would likely alienate many party stalwarts and sour Bradley's prospects of winning the Democratic nomination in the future.

Weicker: A Third Way?

In his recent memoir, Lowell P. Weicker Jr. asserted that the "televised Watergate hearings of the summer of 1973 made [his] a household name for several generations of Americans." Weicker

Lowell P. Weiker Jr.

remained in the Senate for 15 more years and later served as Connecticut's governor from 1991 until 1995, but his national fame proved short-lived. Today, his name is the least widely known among those being bandied about as potential 1996 third-party presidential aspirants.

Only 4 percent of those questioned in an August ABC/*Washington Post* poll said they would take seriously an independent bid by Weicker. Still, Weicker has done what none of his peers has: He has actually won a major office as an independent. Spurned by much of his own state GOP in his unsuccessful Senate re-election campaign in 1988, Weicker won his term as governor two years later on the ticket of his A Connecticut Party.

Weicker, who briefly entered the race for the GOP presidential nomination in 1980, says the chances of his running in 1996 are a "million to one," but he refused to rule out a run categorically while traveling this summer to promote his memoir, *Maverick*.

Weicker spent two decades in Washington after his election to the House in 1968 as a Republican opposed to the Vietnam War. In 1970 he won his first Senate term. He was defeated in 1988 by Democrat Joseph I. Lieberman.

Weicker's standing in the GOP never recovered after his attacks on President Richard M. Nixon from his perch on the Senate Watergate Committee in 1973. He clashed frequently with fellow Republicans, particularly Jesse Helms of North Carolina, and he opposed President Ronald Reagan's cuts in social spending.

Weicker expresses concern that the party has been taken over by "the Johnny-come-lately right-wing moralizing nuts." He says there is a gap in the center that cries out for representation. He also accuses the two major parties of colluding to maintain power.

He says he would like to see the federal budget balanced in three to five years, rather than the seven- and ten-year timetables that congressional Republicans and the White House are debating.

Robert Dornan

California Rep. Robert K. Dornan has never had much trouble attracting attention. His speeches on the House floor have brought cheers from Republican colleagues while bringing Democrats to their feet in a rage. But Dornan's efforts to push his agenda as a candidate for the 1996 GOP presidential nomination are getting lost in a field of contenders actively currying favor with the party's core conservatives.

Dornan has acknowledged the quixotic nature of his campaign. In a July 7 interview he said he might yet seek re-election to the House in 1996, despite earlier statements to the contrary. He also has talked of launching a national talk show, which would give him a forum to help the eventual GOP nominee. He has been a popular fill-in for conservative radio talk show host Rush Limbaugh.

For now, Dornan has vowed to "hang in (the presidential race) as long as I can." Dornan has said that Senate Majority Leader Bob Dole of Kansas has "lapped the field," while he languishes near the end of the pack and draws only a few percentage points in national polls.

A Conservative Campaign

From the outset, Dornan, 62, kept his expectations modest. When he launched his campaign April 13 he said that "winning is not everything" and that he wanted to "contribute to the strength" of the country and advance the issues. But Dornan has had less influence on the race than he might have hoped. Distracted by the Republican resurgence in Washington and near ground zero in

Dornan is a vocal opponent of abortion rights and an outspoken critic of President Clinton.

fundraising, he has campaigned relatively little and garnered scant media attention. On the issues, he has been overshadowed by conservative commentator Patrick J. Buchanan, whose comments over the years have stirred almost as much ire as Dornan's.

"To a degree, his presence seems to be diminished," said American Conservative Union President David A. Keene, who is backing Dole.

David Mason, a political analyst at the Heritage Foundation, a conservative think tank, attributed Dornan's problems to the success of Buchanan and the emergence of conservative talk show host Alan Keyes, whose campaign is also focusing on social issues.

Like Dornan, Buchanan is a vocal opponent of abortion rights and has attacked gay rights.

Brian Bennett, a former aide to Dornan, said he believes Dornan has had some impact on the race. Dornan, "in concert with other people and others in the Christian right . . . have reasserted the primacy of social issues on the Republican agenda."

A Voice Against Clinton

Dornan also is likely to reprise his 1992 role as an acerbic critic of President Clinton, whom he has labeled a "womanizer-adulterer" and "a triple draft dodger." Earlier this year, Dornan said on the House floor that Clinton had lent "aid and comfort to the enemy" by organizing protests against the Vietnam War when he was a student abroad.

Lines such as these, broadcast via C-SPAN or on national radio and TV talk shows, have brought Dornan a national following.

"Bob Dornan, because he's willing to speak out, has a following among a respectable number of people in our society," said Rep. Dana Rohrabacher, R-Calif., whose district borders Dornan's 46th. "They are looking for representation that does not compromise."

A former Air Force pilot, actor and talk show host, Dornan ran unsuccessfully for mayor of Los Angeles in 1973. Three years later, he won a seat in Congress. In 1982, Dornan ran for the Senate, in part because his Santa Monica-based district had lost most of its largely Republican areas in redistricting. Dornan finished fourth in the GOP primary, which Republican Pete Wilson won. Dornan then moved to Orange County and made a comeback in 1984, knocking off a Democratic House incumbent.

The author of a proposed constitutional amendment to ban most abortions, Dornan said that if the 1996 GOP convention in San Diego tries to nominate an abortion-rights candidate for president or vice-president, "San Diego will explode."

While Dornan's focus on social policy stirs his most passionate oratory, he also devotes attention to military issues. He chairs the National Security Subcommittee on Military Personnel and the Intelligence Subcommittee on Technical and Tactical Intelligence, and was a strong supporter of President Ronald Reagan's military buildup in the 1980s and the use of military force in the Persian Gulf in 1991.

Should he choose to stay in Congress, he would have to win another term in a district that is now more than half Hispanic and increasingly Asian. He also could count on being a target for Democrats.

"I don't think anyone particularly takes him seriously, other than those who believe what comes out of his mouth," said James Toledano, chairman of the Orange County Democratic Party.

Thomas A. Fuentes, Orange County GOP chairman, stands by his man: "Whether Bob carries his quest for the White House through all the primaries or if he returns to Orange County, either way, [his campaign] is an issue-oriented message-delivering venture."

Malcolm Forbes Jr.

Malcolm S. "Steve" Forbes Jr., Republican of New Jersey, declared his candidacy in September 1995, long after the rest of the presidential field had developed, but in a sense he could afford to do so. While other candidates began raising money years in advance and struggled to keep the cost of fundraising low, Forbes was able to cover his start-up expenses by depositing $4 million of his own money in his campaign account the month he announced.

The president and chief executive officer of Forbes Inc. since 1990, Forbes, 48, pledged $25 million to his campaign with the same aplomb billionaire Ross Perot brought to paying his own campaign bills in 1992. Because they are not seeking federal matching funds for their efforts, they are free to spend as much as they wish.

Like Perot, Forbes has attracted notice for his ideas and style as well as for his money. He quickly launched a series of short, punchy TV ads that promised a 17 percent flat rate for the federal income tax, with no tax on the first $36,000 for families of four. He followed these with ads attacking front-runner Bob Dole, the Senate majority leader, for his complicity in "$800 billion in tax increases since 1981" and for postponing a Senate floor vote on term limits for members of Congress.

Forbes paints himself as a bold entrepreneur and risk taker who would raise "high the banner of economic expansion and opportunity," as Ronald Reagan did in the 1980s. We need growth, he likes to say, "to enable the two-income family to get ahead of the curve instead of feeling they're on a treadmill."

Buoyed by the ads and by a well-received performance in the candidates' joint TV appearance in Manchester, N.H., in October,

Forbes is a Washington outsider who pledged $25 million of his own money to sustain his campaign.

Forbes shouldered his way into the pack of candidates chasing Dole in the polls. In New Hampshire, he made his debut with 7 percentage points of support, a virtual tie for third with former governor Lamar Alexander of Tennessee and slightly ahead of Sen. Phil Gramm of Texas.

Although lacking previous political experience, Forbes was accorded a measure of respect for his extensive media contacts and his role in financing some of the intellectual activists of the conservative movement in recent years. His candidacy was foretold for months by conservative columnist and TV talk personality Robert Novak.

Forbes was chairman of the board of directors and a major backer for Empower America, which helped keep such figures as former HUD secretary Jack F. Kemp and former education secretary William J. Bennett in the public eye after the administration of President George Bush left Washington. Neither Kemp nor Bennett was willing to run for president in 1996, and neither has yet endorsed Forbes—although both have had lavish praise for the businessman.

A Washington Outsider

Much of what Forbes says on the campaign stump ("It's time to remove the dead weight of Washington, and let the American economy run free") could be from the script of any of the Republican presidential contenders. But he steps out on his own when he espouses a fixed point of value for world currencies, using gold as an example.

He generally dismisses his Republican rivals as insiders who have been "in Washington or in politics or both all of their adult lives" and whose "vision of what we can do is narrow, cramped and constricted."

"I am not an incrementalist," says Forbes, "not a cautious suggester of cautious changes. . . not a compromiser with the bully state."

Forbes has refused to be defined as either pro-choice or pro-life, saying that he supports access to abortion in the early stage of pregnancy but wants to foster a climate in which abortions would be eliminated.

He refuses to acknowledge a downside to his lack of political experience. "The most effective presidents have not always had the fattest political resumes," he said.

The Forbes Name

Forbes is among the nation's wealthiest citizens, but he says that fact will not prevent voters from identifying with him. "Voters will be less concerned about the size of the bankroll than the message," he says.

It was Forbes' grandfather who founded the publishing empire built on the business magazine *Forbes* in 1917. The enterprise passed to Malcolm S. Forbes Sr., who was known as a flamboyant businessman and bon vivant who sometimes squired such glamorous women as Elizabeth Taylor. The elder Forbes died in 1990 (after throwing a last birthday party estimated to have cost $1 million), leaving the far-flung family enterprise of Forbes Inc. to his son and namesake.

Forbes the younger has pursued a far lower profile. Forbes and his wife, Sabina, have five daughters ages 7 to 22. After attending prep school and Princeton University, he entered the Forbes publishing empire and began a career as a volunteer and sometime political activist. He was chairman of the board of International Broadcasting from 1985 until 1993. In 1993, he helped Republican Christine Todd Whitman get elected governor of New Jersey.

Alan Keyes

If Patrick J. Buchanan's function in a presidential race is to crowd other candidates to the right, then Alan Keyes is Pat Buchanan's Pat Buchanan.

"They keep asking me whether I'm going to lose and I'm telling you I don't know," says Keyes. "On any given day of the week, I don't care, either."

A former Reagan administration official who now hosts a radio talk show in Maryland, Keyes has almost no nationwide name recognition and has raised almost no money in his bid for the 1996 GOP presidential nomination. He has twice been a candidate for statewide office in Maryland and been thoroughly drubbed.

He won the national American Legion oratorical contest as a youth, and throughout his career he has been known for being as well-spoken as he is outspoken. "I'm going to go out and I am going to tell it like I think it is," says Keyes, 44, who has found receptive audiences across the country.

Moral issues, especially abortion (which he calls "this moral evil"), form the centerpiece of his campaign. "I do think the moral crisis is the fundamental issue," Keyes said in a recent interview. "Even things like Medicare and Social Security, they really are related to the family system in America," because people turn to the government for help instead of their families.

At a GOP presidential forum in Denver on May 13, Keyes said the federal budget could be balanced "if we make restoring the marriage-based family the No. 1 priority of everything we say and do for the next generation."

Low on Funding

Like Buchanan, Keyes is essentially a commentator who has never held elective office (he served in two appointive jobs in the State Department). If anything, Keyes strives to be even more of an antipolitician than Buchanan, which may be a trait born of necessity as much as design. He raised $50,000 in the first three months of this year, while at least three other presidential aspirants raised $5 million or more.

Keyes has borrowed a page from Buchanan's 1992 playbook, appearing fre-

Keyes's campaign focuses on the moral issues.

quently at Republican events around the country where straw polls are taken. Such votes may not be statistically meaningful, but they are often reported by the media and quoted by campaign workers as signs of grass-roots support.

Keyes fires up crowds almost everywhere he goes, from Georgia to Utah to Oregon. Since he comes off more as a forceful revivalist rather than an ordinary equivocating politician, many listeners respond with unbridled enthusiasm—stomping, cheering and even crying.

Bill Goldsmith, chairman of the Cochise County (Arizona) Republican Party, held a Keyes rally and luncheon in that state April 22. "He went over great," Goldsmith said. "Some of the old retired people who hadn't stood up since the Armistice stood up and cheered."

"I don't change my positions just because my pollster said to. I promise you, this is not just because I can't afford pollsters," Keyes tells a caller to his talk radio program, broadcast from WCBM-AM in Baltimore.

Because of his strong stance against abortion, several members of the Texas State Republican Executive Committee wanted to hand Keyes their endorsement, giving home-state Sen. Phil Gramm a black eye for not hammering the issue hard enough. As a compromise, the party passed a resolution praising Keyes "for his message of values and character."

"Keyes is an impassioned rightist with an almost . . . maniacal commitment to issues [that] people like Gramm have slighted," said Mark Crispin Miller, professor of media studies at Johns Hopkins University.

Keyes accuses Gramm and the campaign's front-runner, Senate Majority Leader Bob Dole of Kansas, of being "expedient, time-serving, finger-in-the-wind politicians" who have tacked on abortion because they are "intimidated by their donors."

Keyes says that his own forthright approach works well with one exception: "I think the main place I get a kind of less than enthusiastic response is when I go to meet with these elite groups of Republican donors."

Friends and Opportunities

Even friendly conservatives such as William Kristol, founder of the Project for the Republican Future, give Keyes no chance of winning the nomination. Kristol was Keyes' roommate at Harvard and ran his first bid for public office. When Republican nominee Thomas L. Blair dropped out of the 1988 Maryland Senate race, the state GOP tapped Keyes to challenge Democratic Sen. Paul S. Sarbanes. Keyes had been recommended by Jeane J. Kirkpatrick, the former U.N. representative whom state party officials had first tried to recruit for the race.

Kirkpatrick had helped Keyes secure jobs in the Reagan administration, first as ambassador to the U.N. Economic and Social Council from 1983 to 1985, then as assistant secretary of state for international organizations from 1985 to 1987. Keyes, a former resident scholar at the American Enterprise Institute, has also been president of Citizens Against Government Waste and interim president of Alabama A&M University.

Keyes received just 38 percent of the vote against Sarbanes, but that did not stop him from challenging Maryland's other Democratic senator, Barbara A. Mikulski, four years later (he finished with 29 percent of the vote).

Miller says that despite his weak record as a candidate in Maryland, Keyes "probably has a natural constituency on the fringes wherever he goes" if only because he is "assured of an exultant reception."

Appendix

How Primaries Work

There are two basic types of presidential primaries. One is the presidential preference primary in which voters vote directly for the person they wish to be nominated for president. The second is the type in which voters elect delegates to the national conventions.

States may use various combinations of these methods:

- A state may have a preference vote but choose delegates at party conventions. The preference vote may or may not be binding on the delegates.
- A state may combine the preference and delegate-selection primaries by electing delegates pledged or favorable to a candidate named on the ballot. Under this system, however, state party organizations may run unpledged slates of delegates.
- A state may have an advisory preference vote and a separate delegate-selection vote in which delegates may be listed as pledged to a candidate, favorable, or unpledged.
- A state may have a mandatory preference vote with a separate delegate-selection vote. In these cases, the delegates are required to reflect the preference primary vote.

For those primaries in which the preference vote is binding upon the delegates, state laws may vary as to the number of ballots through which delegates at the convention must remain committed.

Most primary states hold presidential preference votes, in which voters choose among the candidates who have qualified for the ballot in their states. Although preference votes may be binding or nonbinding, in most states the vote is binding on the delegates, who either are elected in the primary itself or chosen outside of it by a caucus process, by a state committee, or by the candidates who have qualified to win delegates.

Delegates may be bound for as short a time as one ballot or as long as a candidate remains in the race. National Democratic rules in effect in 1980 required delegates to be bound for one ballot unless released by the candidate they were elected to support. The rule was not in effect in subsequent elections.

Until 1980 the Republicans had a rule requiring delegates bound to a specific candidate by state law in primary states to vote for that candidate at the convention regardless of their personal presidential preferences. That rule was repealed at the July 1980 convention.

Delegates from primary states are allocated to candidates in various ways. Most of the methods are based on the preference vote— proportional representation, statewide winner-take-all (in which the candidate winning the most votes statewide wins all the delegates), congressional district and statewide winner-take-all (in which the high vote-getter in a district wins that district's delegates and the high vote-getter statewide wins all the at-large delegates), or some combination of the three. Still another method is the selection of individual delegates in a "loophole," or direct election, primary. Then the preference vote is either nonbinding or there is no preference vote at all.

In the proportional representation system, the qualifying threshold for candidates to win delegates can vary. After a decade of intensive debate, Democratic leaders voted to require proportional representation in all primary and caucus states in 1980. This was made optional in 1984 and 1988, with qualifying thresholds of 20 percent and 15 percent, respectively. For 1992 the Democrats again made proportional allocation mandatory, with candidates awarded delegates if they received 15 percent of the vote. Along with winner-take-all systems, the Democrats also banned winner-reward systems that gave extra delegates to primary or caucus victors.

The Republicans allow the primary states to set their own thresholds, which in many states were lower than the Democrats'. In Massachusetts, for example, a GOP candidate in 1992 had to receive only 2.631 percent of the vote to win a delegate.

In nearly half the primary states, major candidates are placed on the ballot by the secretary of state or a special nominating committee. The consent of the candidate is required in only three states—Kentucky, Michigan, and North Carolina. Elsewhere, candidates must take the initiative to get on the ballot. The filing requirements range from sending a letter of candidacy to elections officials (the case in Puerto Rico) to filing petitions signed by a specified number of registered voters and paying a filing fee (the case in Alabama).

On many primary ballots, voters have the opportunity to mark a line labeled "uncommitted" if they do not prefer any of the candidates.

How Caucuses Work

In the current primary-dominated era of presidential politics, which began two decades ago, caucuses have survived in the quiet backwater of the Democratic nominating process.

Caucuses became controversial in 1984 as they gained in popularity at the expense of presidential primaries. A strong showing in the caucuses by Walter F. Mondale led many Democrats—and not only supporters of his chief rivals—to conclude that caucuses are inherently unfair.

Mondale's caucus victories might be termed the revenge of the insiders. More so than the primaries, the often complex, low-visibility world of caucuses is open to takeover. The mainstream Democratic coalition of party activists, labor union members, and teachers was primed to dominate the caucuses in Mondale's behalf.

The influence of caucuses had decreased in the 1970s as the number of primaries grew dramatically. During the 1960s a candidate sought to run well in primary states mainly to have a bargaining chip with powerful leaders in the caucus states. Republicans Barry M. Goldwater in 1964 and Richard Nixon in 1968 and Democrat Hubert H. Humphrey in 1968 all built up solid majorities among caucus state delegates that carried them to their parties' nominations. Humphrey did not even enter a primary in 1968.

After 1968, candidates placed their principal emphasis on primaries. In 1972, Democrat George McGovern and in 1976 Republican president Gerald R. Ford and Democratic challenger Jimmy Carter won nomination by securing large majorities of the primary state delegates. Neither McGovern nor Ford won a majority of the caucus state delegates. Carter was able to win a majority only after his opponents' campaigns collapsed.

Complex Method

Compared with a primary, the caucus system is complicated. Instead of focusing on a single primary election ballot, the caucus presents a multi-tiered system that involves meetings scheduled over several weeks, sometimes even months. There is mass participation at the first level only, with meetings often lasting several hours and attracting only the most enthusiastic and dedicated party members.

The operation of the caucus varies from state to state, and each party has its own set of rules. Most begin with precinct caucuses or some other type of local mass meeting open to all party voters. Participants, often publicly declaring their votes, elect delegates to the next stage in the process.

In smaller states such as Delaware and Hawaii, delegates are elected directly to a state convention, where the national convention delegates are chosen. In larger states such as Iowa, there is at least one more step. Most frequently, delegates are elected at the precinct caucuses to county conventions, where the national convention delegates are chosen.

Participation, even at the first level of the caucus process, is much lower than in the primaries. Caucus participants usually are local party leaders and activists. Many rank-and file voters find a caucus complex, confusing, or intimidating.

In a caucus state the focus is on one-on-one campaigning. Time, not money, is the most valuable resource. Because organization and personal campaigning are so important, an early start is far more crucial in a caucus state than in most primaries. Because only a small segment of the electorate is targeted in most caucus states, candidates usually use media advertising sparingly.

Although the basic steps in the caucus process are the same for both parties, the rules that govern them are vastly different. Democratic rules have been revamped substantially since 1968, establishing national standards for grass-roots participation. Republican rules have remained largely unchanged, with the states given wide latitude in the selection of delegates. Democratic caucuses are open to Democrats only. Republicans allow crossovers where state law permits, creating a wide range of variations. The first step of the Democratic caucus process must be open, well-publicized mass meetings. In most states Republicans do the same. Generally, voters participate only in the election of local party officials, who meet to begin the caucus process.

Caucus Method

For both the Republican and Democratic parties, the percentage of delegates elected from caucus states was on a sharp decline throughout the 1970s. But the Democrats broke the downward trend and elected more delegates by the caucus process in 1980 than in 1976.

Between 1980 and 1984 six states switched from a primary to a caucus system; none the other way. Since 1984 the trend has turned back toward primaries. In 1992 primaries were held in 38 states, the District of Columbia and Puerto Rico. The Democrats elected 66.9 percent of their national convention delegates in primaries, against only 15.1 percent in caucuses. (The remaining 18.0 percent were "superdelegate" party and elected officials.) The Republicans in 1992 chose 83.9 percent of delegates in primaries and the rest in caucuses, with no superdelegates.

The caucus method came in for widespread criticism in 1988. The Iowa Democratic caucuses were seen as an unrepresentative test dominated by liberal interest groups. The credibility of the caucuses was shaken by the withdrawal from the race of the two winners—Democrat Richard A. Gephardt and Republican Robert Dole—within a month after the caucuses were held. Furthermore, several other state caucuses featured vicious infighting between supporters of various candidates.

In 1992 the presence of a favorite son, Sen. Tom Harkin, among the leading Democratic candidates for president further diminished the Iowa caucus' significance as a rival to the New Hampshire primary as an early indicator of the candidate to beat for the nomination. Harkin easily won his state's party caucus, but he soon dropped out after fading in the primaries elsewhere. By contrast,

20 years earlier, a surprise win in Iowa helped to propel Sen. George McGovern of South Dakota toward the Democratic nomination.

The major complaint about the caucus process is that it does not involve enough voters, and that the low turnouts are not as representative of voter sentiment as a higher-turnout primary.

Staunch defenders, however, believe a caucus has party-building attributes a primary cannot match. They note that several hours at a caucus can involve voters in a way that quickly casting a primary ballot does not. Following caucus meetings, the state party comes away with lists of thousands of voters who can be tapped to volunteer time or money, or even to run for local office. And, while the multi-tiered caucus process is often a chore for the state party to organize, a primary is substantially more expensive.

The Presidential Nominating Process . . .

BEFORE 1968

Party-Dominated

The nomination decision is largely in the hands of party leaders. Candidates win by enlisting support of state and local party machines.

Few Primaries

Most delegates are selected by state party establishments, with little or no public participation. Some primaries are held, but their results do not necessarily determine nominee. Primaries are used to indicate candidate's "electability."

Short Campaigns

Candidates usually begin their public campaign early in the election year.

Easy Money

Candidates frequently raise large amounts of money quickly by tapping a handful of wealthy contributors. No federal limits on spending by candidates.

Limited Media Coverage

Campaigns are followed by print journalists and, in later years, by television. But press coverage of campaigns is not intensive and generally does not play a major role in influencing the process.

Late Decisions

Events early in the campaign year, such as the New Hampshire primary, are not decisive. States that pick delegates late in the year, such as California, frequently are important in selecting nominee. Many states enter convention without making final decisions about candidates.

Open Conventions

National party conventions sometimes begin with nomination still undecided. Outcome determined by maneuvering and negotiations among party factions, often stretching over multiple ballots.

... A Change of Focus

SINCE 1968

Candidate-Dominated

Campaigns are independent of party establishments. Endorsements by party leaders have little effect on nomination choice.

Many Primaries

Most delegates are selected by popular primaries and caucuses. Nominations are determined largely by voters' decisions at these contests.

Long Campaigns

Candidates begin laying groundwork for campaigns three or four years before the election. Candidates who are not well organized at least 18 months before the election may have little chance of winning.

Difficult Fundraising

Campaign contributions are limited to $1,000 per person, so candidates must work endlessly to raise money from thousands of small contributors. PAC contributions are important in primaries. Campaign spending is limited by law, both nationally and for individual states.

Media-Focused

Campaigns are covered intensively by the media, particularly television. Media treatment of candidates plays crucial role in determining the nominee.

"Front-Loaded"

Early events, such as the Iowa caucuses and New Hampshire primary, are important. The nomination may be decided even before many major states vote. Early victories attract great media attention, which gives winners free publicity and greater fundraising ability.

Closed Conventions

Nominee is determined before convention, which does little more than ratify decision made in primaries and caucuses. Convention activities focus on creating favorable media image of candidate for general election campaign.

Index